Mediated Cosmopolitanism

The World of Television News

ALEXA ROBERTSON

polity

First published in 2010 by Polity Press

Polity Press
65 Bridge Street
Cambridge CB2 1UR, UK

Polity Press
350 Main Street
Malden, MA 02148, USA

ISBN-13: 978-0-7456-4947-4
ISBN-13: 978-0-7456-4948-1 (pb)

A catalogue record for this book is available from the British Library.

Typeset in 11 on 13 pt Bembo by
Servis Filmsetting Limited, Stockport, Cheshire.
Printed and bound by MPG Books Group, UK

The publisher has used its best endeavours to ensure that the URLs for external websites referred to in this book are correct and active at the time of going to press. However, the publisher has no responsibility for the websites and can make no guarantee that a site will remain live or that the content is or will remain appropriate.

Every effort has been made to trace all copyright holders, but if any have been inadvertently overlooked the publisher will be pleased to include any necessary credits in any subsequent reprint or edition.

For further information on Polity, visit our website: www.politybooks.com

Contents

List of illustrations

Tables

Figures

Plates

Preface

The world was watching when Barack Obama became US president in 2009. Aware that his inauguration was being followed live by over a billion viewers across the globe, Obama addressed not just Americans, but also the 'other peoples and governments' who were watching that day, 'from the grandest capitals' to the small village in Africa where his father was born. A political scientist sitting with her laptop in front of the television in one such capital (albeit only moderately grand) e-mailed a colleague in Washington and asked what it was like to be there at that moment. The political scientist in Washington replied that she was not in fact experiencing the inauguration with the crowds on the Mall a few blocks from her office, but in front of the television at home. Although they were an ocean and several time zones apart, it transpired that the women were taking part in the historic occasion in virtually the same space, and certainly at the same time.

It may have been unprecedented for the black son of an immigrant to become the president of the most powerful nation on earth, but there was nothing unusual about the experience of the two women. For quite a while, people separated by geography had been sharing events in real time, thanks to developments in communications that had become as ubiquitous as they were rapid.

Most people in the developed world, and many in less developed countries, had come a long way from the nineteenth-century break-fast table at which the man famously depicted by Anderson ([1983] 2006) underwent his ritual of reading the morning newspaper. Anderson's man would meet only a fraction of the other members of his nation, but when he read his paper he did so confident that his fellow citizens were doing the same. By virtue of such routine media consumption, the newspaper-reader had become part of a community of the imagination. It was a national community, and the image of this man is deployed by Anderson in an account of nationalism. A number of scholars, however, have intimated that the image might work when transposed onto a larger canvas.

Television has no borders, as regulators have found, at times to their chagrin; nor should it, in the view of the European Commission.[1] Audiences that have grown steadily in size and geographical scope since Anderson's man opened his paper have watched together as Princess Diana was mourned, as the Twin Towers fell, as people were swept away in the Asian tsunami, as Obama placed his hand on Lincoln's Bible, as Neda died on the streets of Tehran, and as legions of athletes and musicians competed in World Cup football matches and Eurovision song contests.

Such global mediated communion – be it on occasions of political gravitas or when Li Ning lit the Olympic cauldron in Beijing – is a central feature of the process which, according to Beck (2006), is making people cosmopolitans 'by default'. Beck's is a contested claim, and some are troubled by his insistence that it is possible to become a cosmopolitan without being aware of it. But the German sociologist shares with his critics an interest in conscious rather than unconscious or 'latent' forms of cosmopoli-tanism. Whether writing about the preconditions for cosmopolitan democracy, the emergence of a global public or the cultivation of a cosmopolitan awareness, such scholars maintain that, under globalization, citizens must be able, in ordinary ways, to form soli-darities and connections with others who are distant (Stevenson 2003: 97).

This book is about the role that media actors can play in the making of such connections. Its point of departure is that television journalists are among the most powerful of societal sense-makers, and that the stories they tell about the world could help people relate to distant others or lead them to question whether those others *are* so distant after all. But it also explores the possibility that journalists rooted in different media cultures, or speaking to different audiences, may use the semiotic materials circulating in the global mediascape in different ways.

While concerned specifically with the role of the media – or, to be precise, television news – the underlying aim of the book is nevertheless to contribute to the larger scholarly discussion of cosmopolitanism. That discussion has a number of weaknesses.

First, scholars from different fields have had a tendency to talk past each other and often fail to engage with the insights of colleagues who are asking similar questions from different disciplinary vantage points. As Hannerz (2004a, 2005) puts it, there is a 'fault line' between political and cultural understandings of the term, and regrettable blind spots have been the result.

Second, the most significant contributions to the study of cosmopolitanism have, on balance, been theoretical. The empirical work that *has* been done is seldom substantial and – in an age when we are inundated by a plethora of media messages – has been based largely on anecdotal evidence which focuses on distant suffering and conflict.

Third, claims about the preconditions for the development of cosmopolitan consciousness are routinely couched in general terms. Little attention has been paid to how they may vary from one country or culture to another.

While not pretending to overcome such problems, an effort has been made here to avoid compounding them. The focus of the book is on news stories that have both a political and a cultural register, and it thus attempts to integrate insights from both political and cultural conceptions of cosmopolitanism. The study presented in the following pages engages with the substantial literature on cosmopolitanism and other theoretical realms pertinent to the inquiry, but it approaches that literature through an unusual empirical portal.

Scholarship in this field tends to have to do with global issues and a myriad of actors, so it is for good reason that it often takes a bird's-eye view. But the work of imagination does not allow itself to be studied from such a vantage point, at least not empirically. It must be seen close up, and the voices of individual workers of the imagination, and the fruits of their labour, must be made discernible and placed in a meaningful context. For this to be possible, the scope must be radically narrowed. This book focuses on just two sorts of imagination workers – journalists and the people for whom they make news reports – and most of all the stories that are evidence of that imagining. At the same time, the focus is radically expanded in comparison with most other empirical studies of cosmopolitanism, as the insights contributed here are based on the analysis of over 2,000 news reports broadcast on eight different channels, some targeting national and others global audiences. The quantitative analysis of superficial features of those news items has been combined with closer readings of the narrative traits of representative stories.

The book's main thesis is that, if we are to understand how media actors may help make the connections that underpin a cosmopolitan outlook, we must be attentive to evidence that not all do. The point is not that media globalization is a myth, as Hafez (2007) has admittedly good reasons for arguing, but that it is an empirical question. Rather than assuming that global broadcasters are those most liable to foster cosmopolitan ways of seeing and empathizing, we should entertain the possibility that broadcasters targeting national audiences in their safe front rooms (or wherever the screen in current use is situated) might be just as inclined to address their viewers as members of a larger community, or to ask them to imagine such allegiance. If this possibility is to be recognized and explored, it is not enough to look at what is being reported; we should also examine the narrative techniques involved in telling such stories.

The news stories in focus here were broadcast on television. Their selection begs a number of difficult questions. What is television today? And how are the people who use it to be conceived of – as citizens or media consumers; as members of the public or of the audience; or as producers of media texts in their own right?[2] When the Berlin Wall toppled and media globalization was taking off, television was central to the directive governing media policy in Europe. Two decades later, *Television Without Frontiers* was upgraded and became the *Audiovisual Media Services Directive*. The challenge identified by policy-makers was no longer to regulate media production and distribution in an age when satellite broadcasting was demonstrating the porousness of national borders. It was now to retain some degree of control over a mediascape in which 6,500 channels and a host of other digital outlets had become available to Europeans, who could now decide what they wanted to see and when they wanted to see it (Robertson 2010).[3]

While the technological and economic developments reflected in such policy changes are by no means insignificant, the media actors in focus in this book are nevertheless television journalists working for 'traditional' public service broadcasters, targeting national audiences, and mainstream global broadcasters whose moorings are in the public service tradition, even though they rely, to varying degrees, on commercial revenues.[4] They represent continuity, in that most have been operating for decades (and, in the case of the national broadcasters, date back to the days when their viewers had only one channel to watch). But they also represent change, as they have had to adapt to radically altered technological, economic and political circumstances. Ongoing transformations in the media landscape notwithstanding, actors such as these broadcasters continue to play a central role in the sort of processes dealt with here. In times of turbulence and transformation, people continue to turn to familiar faces and voices for interpretation and reassurance.[5] This, at least, is the point of departure for what follows. That most of the channels are based in Northern Europe can be seen as a limitation on the scope of the inquiry. On the other hand, the political and media cultures in which they are based vary in interesting ways, and, while the sample admittedly, and unavoidably, excludes a good part of the world's media cultures, it is nevertheless an antidote to the predominance of studies of Anglo-American media.

The red thread throughout the book is the interplay between three key notions – cosmopolitanism, imagination and narrative – and their relationship to the world portrayed in television news. Chapter 1 introduces them more thoroughly, by reviewing scholarship relevant to each notion and to the study as a whole. Chapter 2 looks at everyday reporting over a period of six weeks in three national and three global channels and examines the narrative techniques that may bring the world closer or keep it at arm's length. In so doing, it explores the role of journalists in the spatial dimension of cosmopolitanization. Chapter 3 takes a closer look at one of the news cultures featured in the preceding chapter, and more specifically at the relationship between the people who report the world, the people for whom the world is reported, and the reports themselves. Chapter 4 contrasts the everyday or 'banal' understandings that were in focus in earlier chapters with news coverage in the ten days following the Asian tsunami, when 'unconscious' or latent cosmopolitanism (following Beck's train of thought) became conscious or active and gave rise, at least momentarily, to a global public. Chapter 5 asks whether cosmopolitanism, and the sort of news narratives that may have a bearing on it, could have a temporal as well as a spatial dimension. It reflects on the finding that history is often invoked when narrating the world of today, and in particular examines its symbolic role in live coverage of the anniversary of a bygone war. Chapter 6 pulls together the threads unravelled in the first five chapters and ends with a question: If we are to make connections with people elsewhere, what should be expected of journalism in the global era?

It is, of course, not only scholars who are concerned about the power of communication and the political work of the imagination. Governmental and non-governmental actors all operate on this wavelength, and it has been said that the contest to control imagery in a global setting is the predominant political struggle of our time. Journalists are also keenly aware of the responsibility that rests on their shoulders (or in their viewfinders, or in the hand that holds the microphone or hovers over the keyboard). The evidence of this is abundant and can be found in programme policy documents, trade publications, training handbooks, interview material and trailers for the channels' own programmes. In one of these, broadcast shortly after operations began in the autumn of 2006, a British journalist working for Al Jazeera English encapsulated the challenge: 'You have to report the world from many different perspectives in order to report the world back to itself.' The question that serves as the leitmotif of the book is: How is that work best done?

Acknowledgements

Ulf Hannerz is a major presence in these pages, and not only because of his theoretical contributions to the study of cosmopolitanism or his initiative in putting together a project team to explore its empirical foundations. Had he not encouraged me, one dark December day, to stick to my idea of presenting my work in the form it takes here, it would have remained a collection of scattered articles and conference papers, obscure to all but the most determined googler. He was also the first reader of the manuscript, which benefited from his comments. Annika Björkdahl, Lilie Chouliaraki, Martin Hall, Maria Hellman, Annabel Herzog, Frank Möller and Kristina Riegert read various parts of the text fragments that preceded that draft; apart from their feedback, their interest in this research was invigorating. The intellectual stimulation and moral support provided by Alexandra Segerberg and Nina Burge, culturally competent political scientists, was more important than they can imagine. I appreciate the time taken and openness shown by the journalists, farmers, librarians, musicians, construction and factory workers and pensioners whose stories form the foundation of chapter 3, which is based on an article previously published in the Swedish *Statsvetenskaplig Tidskrift*. A vote of thanks is due Minna Frydén, Alexandra Martin, Spela Mezik, Helena Onn,

Veronica Persson, Carly Sawyers and Jasmine Tournaj for their patient and altruistic assistance in coding the material reported in chapter 4. The intellectual resources on offer in the classroom are often underestimated and, unbeknown to them, my students at the Department of Political Science at Stockholm University have contributed to this study with their curiosity and enthusiasm. The two wise but anonymous reviewers who read the entire manuscript provided suggestions that not only improved the book but were also a pleasure to follow up on. I am also grateful to Caroline Richmond for her attention to detail, as well as Andrea Drugan at Polity Press for fielding a manuscript that landed, without warning, on her desk late one Friday afternoon, and for providing prompt and encouraging feedback in the months that followed.

Watching television for a living is not always as much fun as one would think, and watching as much as I have was only possible thanks to grants from the Swedish Research Council and the Bank of Sweden Tercentenary Foundation (including an additional grant that made it possible to reproduce the images in plates 1.1, 2.1, 2.3, 2.5 and 5.1, courtesy of BBC News, and plates 2.2, 2.4, 5.2 and 5.3, courtesy of SVT); the support of Claes Linde and Anncristin Länta; the cheerful technical assistance of June Head, Ulrike Klingemann, Michael Lundin and Roland Fredriksson; and, most of all, the wizardry of Bernard Devine, who is the Dumbledore of the Stockholm University Media Library.

Last but not least, I would like to thank my children, Nick and Clarie, for agreeing to share their bedrooms with VCRs and computers that digitize broadcasts day and night, and my husband Claes Åkesson, who struggles valiantly to get the family to pay attention to the news that is unfolding *today*, and not just the old news in the Media Library. It is also largely thanks to Claes that Nick and Clarie are growing up to be cosmopolitans of the actually travelling variety and not just mediascapers. This book is for them.

We were not always burdened by debt, dependent on foreign aid and handouts; in the stories we tell of ourselves we were not the crazed and destitute radicals you see on your television channels but rather saints and poets and – yes – conquering kings.

Mohsin Hamid, *The Reluctant Fundamentalist* (2007)

1

Introduction: Nourishing the Cosmopolitan Imagination

Over half a century ago, Kenneth Boulding suggested that, to understand international relations, it was essential to realize that people respond not to the objective facts of the situation, but to their image of it. 'It is what we think the world is like,' he wrote, 'not what it is really like, that determines our behavior' (Boulding 1959: 120). Central to such responses was the national image, which in his account extended through time, 'backward into a supposedly recorded or perhaps mythological past and forward into an imagined future'. Boulding thought the consciousness of shared events and experiences, of having gone through something together, was of the utmost importance in forming such collective images. But he also thought they could be developed or, as he put it, sophisticated.

> It is akin almost to a Copernican revolution: the unsophisticated image sees the world only from the viewpoint of the viewer; the sophisticated image sees the world from many imagined viewpoints, as a system in which the viewer is only a part. The child sees everything through his own eyes and refers to his own immediate comfort. The adult learns to see the world through the eyes of others; his horizon extends to other times, places and cultures than his own. (Boulding 1959: 130)

At around the same time, the social theorists Harold Innis and Marshall McLuhan were reflecting on how the evolution of the media matters to people's sense of place and belonging. As alluded to in the preface, it is a thought that the political scientist Benedict Anderson developed later. He was by no means alone. John Thompson, a sociologist, later coined the term 'mediated worldliness' to denote how our experience of the world is increasingly shaped by mediated symbolic forms. He maintained that, as our sense of the world and our place in it becomes increasingly nourished by messages circulating in media texts, 'so too our sense of the groups and communities with which we share a common path through time and space, a common origin and a common fate, is altered: we feel ourselves to belong to groups and communities which are constituted in part through the media' (Thompson 1995: 35).

Thompson was not referring to the experiences of passive media consumers, into the empty minds of which broadcasters deposit messages. He, and others working within the hermeneutic tradition, is concerned with what has been called the 'active audience'. The idea is that the consumers of news and other media products actively engage with them, work with them, and create meaning in their meeting with the text, rather than having the message imposed on them. These scholars are in effect writing about the work of the imagination, sometimes implicitly (Ang 1985; Barker 2000; Liebes and Katz 1991; Morley 1980), sometimes explicitly (Appadurai 1996; Boltanski 1999; Chouliaraki 2006, 2008; Delanty 2006; Nava 2007; Silverstone 2007; Stevenson 2003).

While Boulding used the word 'seeing' and Thompson wrote of 'feeling', the verb that will be privileged in what follows is, rather, 'telling'. The creation and maintenance of community is thought by a number of scholars to be one of the leading political uses of narrative. Our identities, insofar as they hinge on our sense of belonging, are not givens. Through the agency of storytelling, our situation in the political and cultural landscape, and that of everyone else, is set out, maintained, negotiated and adapted to new circumstances (Clayton 1994; Coole 1999; Mottier 1999; Mumby 1993; Tambling 1991: 70; Whitebrook 2001: 7–8).

The argument pursued here is that television is a key site for the narrative acts that help us get our bearings in the world and maintain or negotiate a sense of belonging. Television not only has the power required for the imagination of community to which Anderson called our attention; it is also a rich resource in Boulding's process of sophistication – a process which Beck (2006) would be liable to refer to as cosmopolitanization.

One purpose of this chapter is to set out the three key concepts in this book – cosmopolitanism, imagination and narrative – and to consider how they may inform each other. Central to the relation between these concepts is the relation between the political and the cultural. A second purpose is to review work that has addressed that interface and to consider where television comes into the picture (to use an unfortunate phrase). Insights gained from this review of the literature will, finally, be translated into research questions. The chapter ends with a brief account of the method used to find answers to them.

Cosmopolitanism

As mentioned earlier, cosmopolitanism has meant different things in different contexts. For those who consider themselves champions of human rights, the word has positive connotations; for those who consider themselves patriots, it has negative, or at least thin, cold ones. For some, cosmopolitanism is highly controversial: the classic debate invoked in this context is that represented by the contributors to *For Love of Country* (Nussbaum et al. 1996), who are far from achieving a consensus as to whether cosmopolitan and nationalist affinities are mutually exclusive. For someone like Beck, cosmopolitanism is not (just) a matter of what is good or bad, it is simply the way things *are*. It is not without good reason that Brennan (2002, 2003) has remarked that cosmopolitanism is an ambiguous phenomenon.

Two of the adventurous academics who have attempted to sort out the various understandings of the concept are Vertovec and Cohen (2002). They distinguish between six main conceptions: the socio-cultural condition that interests Appadurai; the philosophical take on the world expressed in Beck's cosmopolitan manifesto; the political project to build transnational institutions that Kaldor has written about; the political project to achieve recognition of multiple identities associated with the work of Held; the mode of orientation to the world with which Hannerz is connected; and a set of competences that make it possible for people to get along in other cultures, about which Friedman has written. There is, however, considerable overlap, both between these different conceptions and between the concerns of the afore-mentioned scholars. In *The Cosmopolitan Vision*, for example, Beck writes as much about a condition as a philosophy, and even in his early pieces on the topic Hannerz wrote a good deal about competence. There is much to be said for Delanty's argument (2006: 27) that the very notion makes it necessary to recognize many kinds of cosmopolitanism – a challenge to which Holton (2009) has risen by distinguishing no fewer than seventeen types.

What Delanty has in mind, however, are three broad types of a phenomenon that has to do with how we relate to the world: moral, political and cultural cosmopolitanism. This is not far from the bifurcation identified by Hannerz (2004a, 2005) between political and cultural understandings of it, as the political variety at least has pronounced moral overtones. Because this book has to do with cosmopolitanism as an empirical phenomenon rather than as a normative vision, the moral type will be left to the political philosophers to explore, and the focus in what follows will be on the other two types.

Political cosmopolitanism

According to Held, the new circumstances prevailing under glo-balization compel us to find common frameworks for political action and institutional arrangements. The ethical and political space provided by such frameworks 'sets out the terms of reference for the recognition of people's equal moral worth' (Held 2002: 313). Cosmopolitanism in this conception has to do with defend-ing the right of people to be treated with equal respect, which in turn entails a transnational democracy project that extends beyond the nation-state.

'Weaker' versions of political cosmopolitanism can be found in theories of citizenship. In Benhabib's rendition, cosmopolitanism has to do with furthering multiple and overlapping allegiances in societies that are growing increasingly multicultural. It thus involves sustaining such allegiances across communities of language, ethnicity, religion and nationality (Benhabib 2004: 174–5). The requisite sustenance is to be derived from safeguards to protect the rights of minorities to their own culture and representation, and the rights of all to the information technology on which modern social life is predicated.

Proponents of political cosmopolitanism are concerned with issues of gender, environment, human rights and peace: as Hannerz (2004a) has so pithily observed, it is 'cosmopolitanism with a worried face'. The figure in focus is not just someone with human rights and the right to political representation, however. He or she also has civic obligations, and is familiar as the 'well-informed citizen' at the heart of democratic theory who is expected to keep abreast of developments in the political environment, and to act in a responsible fashion on the basis of that information.

Political cosmopolitanism has been described as 'thin' (Calhoun 2002: 878) and is often seen as an elite project with a 'top-down' trajectory. It thus makes sense that it is often associated, in concrete applications, with the project of the European Union, which has yet to succeed in engaging the hearts and minds of its inhabitants. But the claims of political cosmopolitanism transcend the regional: as one of its foremost proponents (Habermas 2001) has argued, only the development of a genuinely global civil society and public sphere will foster the development of cosmopolitan solidarity. It is at this point that the political merges with the cultural.

Cultural cosmopolitanism

Stevenson (2003) has drawn attention to the relationship between the practice of politics and an increasingly 'symbolic' society. In order to understand that relationship, he says, it is not enough to explore the political itself. There is a relationship between culture and globalization to be addressed, and cause to consider the cultural dimension of cosmopolitanization.

Schirato and Webb (2003) are two of the writers who maintain that globalization should be considered in terms not only of politics (and economics and technology) but also (and perhaps primarily) of culture. Invoking Bourdieu and Bauman, they argue that the changes we need to understand are located within powerful discourses that shape everyday life, discourses which simultaneously name, and thus help to bring into being what they are supposedly designating or describing' (Schirato and Webb 2003: 9). Writers such as these urge us to shift our analytical gaze from ideas and political projects to discourses and everyday practices. This is the realm of culture.

World culture, according to Hannerz, is not about reproducing uniformity but about organizing diversity. His cosmopolitan is someone who has developed the competence to do such work, who can respect and deal with such diversity, and who is willing to engage with the Other. Cosmopolitanism in this version 'is an intellectual and aesthetic stance of openness toward divergent cultural experiences, a search for contrasts rather than uniformity' (Hannerz 1990: 239). Cultural competence is important to the study reported in this book. It is not a simple notion, however: it has two sides, both of which are activated when the subject matter is media texts and audiences. The challenge is to be able to discern the meanings that culturally competent audience members develop out of media discourse, and which comprise one dimension of the communicative relationship that journalists have with their readers, listeners and viewers. But the challenge also involves keeping an eye on how such media work may help audience members *develop* competence at manoeuvring in cultures with which they are less familiar, and which may become less strange through increased exposure.

Connectivity is a key term in Tomlinson's influential account of globalization and culture, which he ends by asking what it means 'to have a global identity, to think and act as a "citizen of the world" – literally as a "cosmopolitan"' (Tomlinson 1999: 184). Taking Hannerz's cosmopolitan as his point of departure, he adds some requirements. To merit the name, a cosmopolitan needs to have a sense of wider cultural commitment (ibid.: 186), an active experience 'of belonging to the wider world', and an identity 'that embraces a sense of what unites us as human beings, of common

risks and possibilities, of mutual responsibilities' (ibid.: 194). At
the same time (and here he is on the same wavelength as Hannerz
when the latter writes about the propensity to organize diversity),
the cosmopolitan must have 'an awareness of the world as one of
many cultural others' (ibid.). This awareness must be reflexive,
which means that people must be open to questioning their own
cultural assumptions and myths. Tomlinson acknowledges the
tension that exists between these attributes, but argues that they are
nevertheless 'mutually tempering' and (if his idea is to be translated
into the sort of terminology used earlier) part of the negotiation
involved in identity work.

Szerszynski and Urry continue the discussion and ask how a
wider awareness of the world might be altering the nature of local
feelings of belonging, and what role the media play in the production and maintenance of cosmopolitan attitudes to the 'wider
world' (Szerszynski and Urry 2002: 462; see also Holton 2009: 44).
In their view, a cosmopolitan predisposition involves extensive
mobility. This need not be physical or, as they put it, 'corporal'; it
could be virtual or imaginative. It involves curiosity about many
places, peoples and cultures; a willingness (familiar from Hannerz's
account) to take risks by encountering the Other; semiotic skills to
interpret images of various others; and 'an ability to "map" one's
own society and its culture in terms of a historical and geographical
knowledge, to have some ability to reflect upon and judge aesthet-
ically between different natures, places and societies' (Szerszynski
and Urry 2002: 470). Cosmopolitanism, seen in cultural terms, has
to do with inhabiting the world at a distance (Szerszynski and Urry
2006: 115).

Nava (2007) has also written of corporal or, as she puts it, 'visceral' engagement with the other. But she takes writers such as
Szerszynski, Urry and Hannerz to task for assuming (presumably
unconsciously) that the cosmopolitan is a man, and for focusing
on distance and on the activity of seeing the world from afar.
Cosmopolitanism, in her historically informed account, is a structure of feeling that can have a local incarnation and be rooted in
the everyday: it is 'not only visceral and vernacular but also domestic' (Nava 2007: 12).

Political and cultural understandings of cosmopolitanism coincide in the notion of citizenship. In the political version, citizenship has to do with the right to belong and with the obligation to keep informed about matters of concern to the wider community. In the cultural version, it has to do with the right to information and to develop the competence to deal with that information – to understand – and with an obligation to use that information and understanding in a way that promotes solidarity with others, even if they are distant or different. Seen from a cultural perspective, these rights and obligations are not just connected to information. They have to do with images, visuality and meaning as well – if not more so. Cosmopolitan citizenship thus has to do with 'a transformation of vision' (Szerszynski and Urry 2006: 115).

Television and cosmopolitanism

It should already be clear that the media in general, and television in particular, have a lot to do with cosmopolitanism. Loshitsky (1996) sees television as a site of travel. For Thompson (1995) and Barker (1999), it is a site of popular knowledge about the world. And, a decade before the world attended Obama's inauguration, Meyrowitz (1999) was already interested in how television was altering the 'situational geography' of social life, so that people had through its auspices come to inhabit a worldwide space in which new forms of identification could be forged. Reversing the gaze some years later, Nava (2007: 13) saw the intimate form of the television medium as cumulatively generating 'in the familiar domestiscape of the living room, an increasing deterritorialisation of the globe by normalising difference'. Whether opening a window and letting the viewer climb out to explore distant realms, as in the Meyrowitzian version, or letting the world come in and snuggle up beside the viewer on the couch, as in Nava's account, television would seem to have a bearing on cosmopolitanism.

Barker's argument is that television, as it spreads globally, is a major and proliferating resource for the construction of cultural identities, of which a cosmopolitan identity could be considered one. He uses the term 'resource' on purpose, to indicate that television is actively appropriated and deployed by audiences: it provides 'materials to be worked on', he says (Barker 1999: 7). Apart from its content, Szerszynski and Urry (2006: 121–2) maintain that television has certain formal characteristics that could displace 'unreflective identification with local and national cultures' and place them in a wider context, thereby facilitating encounters with various global 'others'. In their view, contemporary cosmopolitanism 'has developed in and through imaginative travel through the TV' (Szerszynski and Urry 2002: 470). They are two of the scholars who have an articulated interest in the relationship between cosmopolitanism and television.[1] To their names must be added those of Cottle and Rai, and Chouliaraki.

Inspired by Heidegger, and in particular his 1919 comment that the radio had transformed his little world, Szerszynski and Urry consider how television as well as radio 'de-severed the local, national and global worlds' and transformed not just Heidegger's but 'all our "little worlds"'. As they see it, cosmopolitanism is a globalization 'in the head', and global imagery is helping people conceive of the world as a whole. What makes their work of particular interest here is their focus on cosmopolitanism in its 'thicker' form and on how it may be developed on a routine basis, through mediations of people and places that are 'folded into our daily lives'. They argue that, while Robert Putnam has a point when he complains that television may be eroding local belonging and involvement, it could nevertheless be good for belonging and involvement at the global level. What is important about television is its agency in circulating symbolic resources: 'It circulates images and narratives – images of places, brands, peoples and the globe itself, and narratives of various figures, heroes and organisations' (Szerszynski and Urry 2002: 465).Theirs is a radical view of the transformative power of electronic media. Szerszynski and Urry remain unconvinced when Habermas insists that face-to-face dialogue is essential to a functioning public sphere, and suggest that it is being transformed by the mediated nature of contemporary social life. Drawing on Thompson, they argue that the media induce an 'enforced proximity' that is relevant to cosmopolitanism.

The encounters of Szerszynski and Urry with traditional notions of the public sphere and related avenues of inquiry are refreshing, and the research questions they pose are compelling. It is also encouraging that they attempt to find answers to such questions through empirical investigation. It is, on the other hand, regrettable that the conclusions they draw about transformations, enforced proximity and the agency of television rest on an insubstantial footing. Although they have combined focus groups and interviews with journalists with textual analysis – the approach taken in this book – the media texts they have examined comprise a small amount of material. One of their studies, for example, surveyed all the visual images available on several television channels – but in only one country (the UK) and over one 24-hour period (Szerszynski and Urry 2002: 466). It was a good start, but the insights yielded by the study are difficult to generalize.

The same must be said of work by Chouliaraki (2006, 2008), who asks whether the media enable the expansion of moral imagination beyond existing communities of belonging, be they national or regional. Reviewing the case for (the 'optimists') and against (the 'pessimists'), she concludes that television – or, as she puts it, satellite broadcasting – brings distant suffering closer to us and maximizes it on our television screens, but it does so in an ambivalent manner (Chouliaraki 2008: 332).

Chouliaraki explores what she calls the symbolic process of the imagination of community in television news by focusing on six case studies of news on suffering. Four of these relate, she says, to communitarian publics, while two are evidence that the Eurocentric imagination can be expanded if the visibility of suffering is managed in non-routine ways. In her analysis, she examines two categories of reports: 'ordinary news' (the stories we hardly ever remember) and 'extraordinary' news (stories that are hard to forget). There is a point to making this distinction, although I think it imprudent to assume that we forget ordinary news: I would argue (and will indeed do so in what follows) that we remember the narrative themes and frameworks into which ordinary news stories are placed.

Despite their differences, ordinary and extraordinary news stories share a key feature, according to Chouliaraki (2008: 338–9): 'they address their audiences, both national and international, as an already constituted community. This is a community that is united in blocking out emotions for "irrelevant" suffering or united in fully empathizing with sufferers who are "like us".' The question she fails to pose is: Who do different media say are like us?

Chouliaraki's work is theoretically rich but leaves much unexplored in the empirical dimension. It also has an articulated normative interest where, as has already been made clear, the question guiding this study is whether cosmopolitan things *are* happening, not whether they *should* be happening. While her focus is on ideal types, applied to a small number of news items, I want to explore a larger body of material and look at more than news of suffering. Chouliaraki lacks empirical evidence to support her conclusion that neither emergency nor ordinary news 'provides us with a quality of connectivity that brings with it a responsibility towards suffering outside Western communities of belonging' (2008: 339). And when she implicitly disagrees with Szerszynski and Urry by claiming that television may be broadcasting globally but media outlets still 'remain within their own particular worlds', she does so without the empirical evidence they deploy to reach the opposite insight. Nevertheless, her contribution to the debate is a valuable one, not least the point she makes that neither the optimists nor the pessimists have engaged in a systematic examination of 'the symbolic properties of satellite broadcasting'. And she is convincing when she observes that it is difficult to identify the cultural resources – i.e. 'aesthetic registers and ethical discourses' – through which television news stories contribute to the sort of collective dispositions that matter to cosmopolitanism.

Cottle and Rai (2008) ask the same sort of questions as Chouliaraki, and also compare the claims of the optimists and the pessimists, but they differ in their emphasis on the need for empirical analysis to back up such claims, as well as other claims about whether media developments are characterized by continuity or change. Their research is of particular interest to the present study because Cottle and Rai acknowledge that 'there is a communicative complexity in the different structures that routinely deliver television news', and because they choose to grasp that complexity through empirical analysis rather than subsume it in theoretical generalization.

Cottle and Rai provide an insightful critique of the trajectory of work on the media and cosmopolitan connectivity. If, they argue, the Vietnam War was the first television war, then the article published by Galtung and Ruge in 1965 was the first significant work in the field of global media studies, whether or not the Norwegians were aware of it. Cottle and Rai applaud Galtung and Ruge for having identified structures of foreign news reporting which conditioned the values which in turn determined what parts of the world would be drawn to the attention of newspaper readers on a given day. But Galtung and Ruge failed to consider that *how* the news was reported could also be worth looking at, and Cottle and Rai are not alone in finding this a weakness. The UNESCO debates of the 1970s, the MacBride report of 1980, and theories of media and cultural imperialism also fall short of the mark, in the view of Cottle and Rai, as they consider information flows from a macro-level of abstraction and say little about how particular voices, from various parts of the world, feature in these flows. The arguments of the political economists – that today's rich media produce poor democracy – and of scholars such as Thussu, who is concerned that the global newsroom is becoming increasingly entertainment-driven, do not rest on detailed empirical engagement. Others are so preoccupied by the quality of liveness of global news reporting that they fail to attend to the considerable differences between the outlets responsible for that reporting. Both the global public sphere theorists and cosmopolitans such as Ingrid Volkmer, Ulf Hannerz and James Lull make claims based on 'limited empirical engagement' (Cottle and Rai 2008: 159–63).

Cottle and Rai (and Cottle 2009) call for research that maps out how different communicative structures could help sustain bonds of solidarity. The key concept here is 'communicative frames', or 'the established repertoire of communicative structures', on which journalists draw in their reports. These can be discursively 'open' or 'closed'. Responding to their own challenge, Cottle and Rai conducted analyses of global broadcasts in which they found that television news contained a number of 'consensual frames' that are based more on cultural display than on reporting information and which 'work at a more culturally expressive level, visually displaying resonant symbols, affirming communal identities and values or recycling cultural myths' (Cottle and Rai 2008: 167).

In the material they examine, they find some communicative frames which they consider able to display and 'valorize' cultural difference by communicating 'something of the lived experiences of distant others or elaborating analyses and discussion that provide "thick descriptions of reality"' – frames, in other words, which could be thought relevant to an understanding of cosmopolitanization processes. They conclude that:

> it is time to engage much more closely and empirically with exactly how disparate conflicts and cultural differences around the world are publicly enacted and elaborated in and through the communicative structure of global news channels. Only then will we be able to arrive at a more considered and evidence-based evaluation of global news output and performance and its potential contribution to communicative democracy. (Cottle and Rai 2008: 177)

Stevenson also finds communication and democracy, like culture and citizenship, to be inextricably linked. If cultures are no longer assumed to be homogeneous and national by definition – a not unreasonable assumption in the twenty-first century – then it no longer makes sense to prioritize the link between the nation and the citizen. Stevenson is interested in the exploration of 'different, less "organic" and more fluid and contested metaphors' and perceives a need to be able to distinguish discourses that foster cosmopolitan solidarity from those that simply homogenize difference (Stevenson 2003: 16, 29). To talk of cultural citizenship in a cosmopolitan context, he argues, using different language from Cottle and Rai but with the same thing in mind, means developing an appreciation of the ways in which 'ordinary' understandings become constructed (ibid.: 4).

Silverstone developed the notion of 'mediapolis' to describe the moral space in which such construction work takes place: a space 'in which the world appears and in which the world is constituted in its worldliness, and through which we learn about those who are and who are not like us' (Silverstone 2007: 31). His vision is explicitly cosmopolitan, and his concern is with 'mediators between the present and immediate realities of everyday life and the world which is spatially and temporally beyond immediate reach' (ibid.:

45). Like all others, Silverstone's cosmopolitan is mobile. What interests him, however, is symbolic rather than physical mobility. Although Silverstone claims that the threads of his argument are phenomenological, sociological, political and technological, his version of the relationship between the media and cosmopolitanism is essentially a cultural one, in the sense used here, and one of obligation. While it is not a term he uses, it could be argued that inhabiting Silverstone's mediapolis in effect entails cultural citizenship. It certainly entails reflecting upon how the other is viewed and how such a vision is constructed.

The empirical study upon which this book is based seeks to develop the sort of appreciation that Stevenson, Cottle and Rai, and Silverstone have, in one way or another, been calling for. The argument pursued in the following pages is that 'imagination' is entailed in this, and that storytelling is intrinsic to the construction work alluded to. Cosmopolitanism in what follows has to do with the preconditions for cosmopolitan citizenship, which in turn is seen as having both political and cultural components. It involves both rights and obligations, both information and understanding. It has to do with what Delanty (2006: 36) has called the dynamic relation between the local and the glocal, with belonging in a world of overlapping allegiances. These allegiances are to people who inhabit the same locality, nation, region or world.

How these dimensions are defined is something best established empirically, as the definitions are to be found in banal cultural discourse. That is where the work of the imagination, and of storytelling, comes in.

Imagination

Arendt was perhaps the first to introduce the notion of imagination into the sort of discussion that now takes place under the rubric of cosmopolitanism. Imagination, she famously wrote, is what makes it possible for us to see things in their proper perspective – neither too close, because understanding requires 'proper distance', nor too far. Remoteness must be bridged 'until we can see and understand everything that is too far away from us as though it were our own affair' (Arendt 1994: 323).

Appadurai was later to argue that imagination has become social practice and is 'the key component of the new global order'. The building blocks of what he calls 'imagined worlds' are five dimensions of global cultural flows. These are the by now famous 'scapes' – ethnoscapes, technoscapes, financescapes, ideoscapes and mediascapes. The last of these, in Appadurai's account, offer repertoires of images and narratives that can be used in making sense of our lives and those of others (Appadurai 1996: 33–5).

Identity is a way of imagining, according to Barker (1999: 6). Nationhood, for example, is 'a symbolic and communicative device around which people can imagine themselves to be one and to identify with their neighbours' (ibid.: 5). But imagining the nation is a less compelling focus of research in a world in which physical and virtual borders are dissolving than the cosmopolitan imagination, which has come to interest a growing number of scholars (Brennan 2002; Chouliaraki 2006, 2008; Delanty 2006; Stevenson 2003; Szerszynski and Urry 2006). Delanty, for example, writes about how:

> the global public impinges upon political communication and other kinds of public discourse creating as a result new visions of social order. To speak of cosmopolianism as real [. . .] is thus to refer to these situations, which we may term the cosmopolitan imagination, where the constitution of the social world is articulated through cultural models in which codifications of both Self and Other undergo transformation. (Delanty 2006: 37)

He notes elsewhere that the power of community is strongly related to cultural discourse and to the definitions, principles and cognitive models that emerge for imagining the world. The power of community, he argues, is essentially the power of communication (Delanty 2003: 157).

Stevenson agrees, and asks us to pay attention to the control of the powerful over dominant discourses and frameworks of understanding. It is, he insists, a key structural division in the world of today (Stevenson 2003: 17). Invoking Castells (1997), who tells us that 'sites of this power are people's minds', Stevenson argues that how we address the issues of cosmopolitanism depends on 'shifting discourses and narratives' that have become available in various contexts (Stevenson 2003: 5). His is a normative as well as a scholarly concern: he is interested in how we might provide fertile ground for the cosmopolitan imagination. As should be clear by now, mine is an empirical concern: I am interested not in how 'we' might provide this ground, but in how journalists can and sometimes do.

To write of the control of people's minds by the powerful is to summon images of propaganda, not least at times of crisis and war – for example, in the years in which the 'war on terror' has raged. It is important to be clear at this stage that the discourses and frameworks of understanding at the heart of this book are of the more banal variety (if I may join the chorus that can't resist reprising Billig's catchy jingle; Billig 1992). The concern here is with the steady drip of images and stories that could shape understandings of the world in unspectacular, and thus often unnoticed, ways.

'We may read,' says Ettema (2005: 131), 'even in the mundane stories of daily journalism, important truths about the cultural constitution of our world.' Carey (1989) urges us to think of news consumption in terms of ritual. Understood in this way, opening the morning paper or sitting down in front of the television in time for the main evening newscast is not so much about learning something new as about confirming what is already known about the world. Carey equates this activity with attending mass.

The two functions (learning something new and confirming what is already known in a daily ritual) have an uneasy coexistence and yet are not mutually exclusive. A musician may spend half an hour each day practising scales and etudes in familiar keys and with established time signatures, but this daily routine usually has the purpose of increasing the musician's skill and confidence, and of thereby acquiring the competence needed to tackle an unfamiliar piece of music by a new composer in a key not previously mastered. In a similar way, a person may consume the daily news in a routine or ritual fashion (the cultural dimension), while at the same time developing the information resources and cognitive competence needed to deal with new information or data, as it will be referred to below (the political or civic dimension). News consumption, in other words, is about using old understandings to comprehend changing circumstances such as those of an increasingly globalized world. The well-informed citizen (in the moments in which people play this role) is given insights by journalists into new developments and people and places with which he or she may be unfamiliar. The ritual of viewing provides the instruments, or cultural repertoire, to make sense of these novelties. Such a repertoire consists of frameworks of understanding, myths, values and narrative themes (on which more later) that are rehearsed and reworked in what Vivian Martin (2008) calls the daily news 'regimen'.

This sort of imaginative work is the key to what Ettema (2005) refers to as 'cultural resonance'. He is interested in how the recurrence of formal textual features in news reporting projects 'cultural power' and thereby helps constitute the 'public and cultural relation among object, tradition and audience' (Ettema 2005: 134).

> The news, like other forms of media, enables and directs the gaze of its audience upon others. Through that gaze others are evaluated and differences between self and others are recognized [. . .] Acts of plural reflexivity, whether religious ritual or newspaper editorial, are acts of cultural self-definition. While anthropologists have often celebrated the role of reflexivity in maintaining the bonds of tribal societies, mass-mediated societies also seek a meaningful sense of self. (Ettema 2005: 143)

Reflexive acts, he says, make our familiar world strange without rendering it incomprehensible. The question posed here is whether, and how, they may also make strange worlds familiar and understandable.

Although working in a different tradition, Brewer (2006) is also interested in cultural power and resonance in news reporting. He points to how political leaders, media actors and ordinary citizens all draw on a variety of frames to explain world affairs. But he maintains that not all frames wield the same power: the languages and ideas of some frames resonate more profoundly in a given political culture, and consequently have an advantage over others

(Brewer 2006: 90). In a study of what he calls 'national interest' frames, Brewer found that, when another nation was framed as a competitor to the interests of the home nation, people viewed that nation less favourably. He also found that when the media framed another nation as either sharing national interests or willing to contribute to them, the nation was viewed more favourably (ibid.: 98). In a later chapter, this insight will be revisited and applied to a cosmopolitan rather than a(n) (inter)national setting, and more specifically to the reporting of an event that depicted the interests of a larger, somewhat vaguely defined community, sixty years after the Second World War. The power of the frames deployed on that occasion derives, at least in part, from the reluctance or inability to define which community beyond the nation had shared interests. As will be seen in chapter 5, the framing also had varying cultural resonance.

At issue here is considerably more than framing. Media enactment, performance, image and affect are also in play, as Cottle and Rai suggest. Here again the political and the cultural coincide. Theorists such as Benhabib, Dryzek and Habermas have argued that public deliberation about values is fundamental to democratic processes at any level. Cottle and Rai applaud them for broadening conceptions of political communication in this way, and for the insight that having the imagination to understand the other and to live with difference is essential if people are to get along in culturally diverse societies. But Cottle and Rai find fault with these theorists (with the partial exception of Habermas) because of their failure to acknowledge that the media have a central role to play in processes of public deliberation – processes that are not just political, involving reason, speech and analysis, but also, given their performative dimension, cultural. Public deliberation about fundamental values in culturally diverse societies is also encouraged by 'dramatic re-enactments, visualised narratives, experiential accounts and emotive testimonies' (Cottle and Rai 2008: 165–6). The work of imagination underpinning cosmopolitanism thus involves making connections across time as well as space. The triggering of recall and memory in the viewer, and the meanings he or she might give to accounts of the outside world, is widely thought to entail a form of power.

Price (1995) claims that political influence over imagery is historical fact; what he and others such as Chalaby (2007) suggest is new(er) is the way in which the fates of governments are 'inextricably intertwined' with the structure and capacity of communications. As difficult as it may be, he writes, states keep struggling to maintain a monopoly over imagery: 'The millions of images that float through the public mind help determine the very nature of national allegiances, attitudes towards place, family, government and the states [. . .] Communal symbols reinforce cohesion' (Price 1995: 3). Put differently, the question is how discourses relating to communal cohesion, which encourage or discourage the making of connections, can be generated and sustained. Writing in 1995, Price was interested in how the state could succeed with this imaginative work. A decade and a half deeper into globalization, it is more pertinent to ask how actors other than abstract 'states' may be dealing with the challenge in a world where national allegiances are not the only ones calling for cohesion and drawing on symbolism in their narrative work.

Narrative

According to Peffley and Hurwitz (1992), people are compelled to use simplification strategies, or heuristics, to make sense of a complex international domain. Given that perceptions of the former Soviet Union (the heuristic of the image of the enemy) had been found to structure specific policy beliefs held by Americans, Peffley and Hurwitz asked what happened when such images changed. They found that images both affect, and are affected by, new information from the world beyond the nation. Such responses, they argued, should be viewed in terms of a hierarchical model of attitude constraint, according to which general beliefs (images of international actors) constrain specific policy preferences (such as support for armed intervention or negotiated solutions to conflict). People, they concluded, are both 'theory-driven' and 'data-driven'.

What Peffley and Hurwitz understand as 'theory' is akin to what is in mind here when the word 'narrative' is invoked – or, more precisely, the notion of narrative understanding.

It has already been suggested, in earlier sections of this chapter, that the work of the imagination has to do with power – political, cultural and discursive. Meaning is made in the context of certain constellations of power, and Mumby (1993: 6–7) thus emphasizes the importance of understanding how people 'are more readily able to accept some "realities" than others and sometimes become imprisoned by those realities'. Similarly, Bruner talks of how we 'cobble stories together to make them into a whole of some sort', and of the accumulation of narratives into cultures, histories or traditions. This involves capacities for gathering stories that permit continuity from the past to the present and the shoring up of traditions (Bruner 1991: 18–20). These and other scholars have emphasized the value of paying attention to 'stories that particular cultures tell and to which their members listen' (Carlisle 1994: 10).

For a long time, narrative was a method used mainly by historians, who sorted out the chaos of past events, and often filled in blanks left by missing evidence, by organizing their primary source material into stories. This sort of work is sometimes referred to as the narrative mode of representing knowledge. Then came what has been referred to as the 'narrative turn', and scholars began instead to argue that social life itself – and not just accounts of it – is a matter of stories, and that our identities and actions come into being through the telling of tales.

Among those who took part in the narrative turn were scholars from the fields of political science, sociology, organization studies, anthropology, linguistics, gender studies, psychology, education, law, biology and physics. Even some historians, who had abandoned narrative in the search for more rigorous methods of analysis, showed a rekindled interest in this approach. The concept of narrative ceased to be the 'epistemological other' of the social sciences, as it once had been (Somers 1994: 613).

What had made it the Other was the distinct contrast it formed to empiricism and quantitative methods of analysis. Narrativists tended to show an interest in the particular story rather than in the general patterns to be found in large amounts of data. The emphasis in their work was interpretation rather than quantification. Four national traditions influenced the development of literary narrative analysis: Russian formalism, American new criticism, French structuralism and German hermeneutics (Polkinghorne 1987). Given such a colourful background, it is hardly surprising that we lack what Riessman would call a binding theory of narrative: like cosmopolitanism, the study of narrative is characterized by great conceptual diversity (Riessman 1993: 17).

The assumptions underpinning narrative studies are perhaps the one thing on which scholars are most agreed. Although expressed variously, they boil down to the view that we organize our experience mainly in the form of narrative (Bruner 1991; Czarniawska 1999, 2000, 2004; Giddens 1991; Somers 1994; Larsen 2002; Lieblich et al. 1982). 'People use stories to entertain, to teach and to learn, to ask for an interpretation and to give one,' writes Czarniawska (2000: 2). For that reason, anyone interested in social life, 'no matter of which domain, needs to become interested in narrative as a form of knowledge, a form of social life and a form of communication'. Similarly, Larsen tells us that narrative works as a fundamental interpretive frame, helping people to organize their experiences and make their world understandable (Larsen 2002: 123).

Somers is also of the view that experience is constituted through narratives. 'People are guided to act in certain ways and not others on the basis of the projections, expectations and memories derived from a repertoire of available social, public and cultural narratives' (Somers 1994: 614). To understand better the assumptions underlying her view of narrative, it is helpful to see how she contrasts it with a traditional analysis of action, which sees people as rational actors motivated by means–ends preferences. A narrative identity approach differs because it assumes that 'people act in particular ways because *not* to do so would fundamentally violate their sense of *being* at that particular time and place' (ibid.: 624). MacIntyre sees our actions and words as becoming intelligible only within a narrative setting. It is through stories that others can understand what our words and actions mean (MacIntyre in Stephenson 1999: 3). Stories, say Lieblich and her colleagues, shape and even construct the personality and reality of the narrator. 'We know or discover ourselves, and reveal ourselves to others, by the stories we tell' (Lieblich et al. 1982: 7).

One reason for studying narratives is to learn more about the power to regulate understandings in society and, related to that, to learn about identity and about how people make sense of the world around them (Lieblich et al. 1982; Mottier 1999; Riessman 1993; Somers 1994). This makes narrative analysis particularly pertinent to the study of cosmopolitanism.

The individual is obviously not divorced from the collective, and, if they can give us insights into sense-making on the individual level, narratives are presumably of value when understanding collectivities as well. Consequently, one reason given by many scholars for studying narrative (even if they don't all put it quite in these terms) is to fill a gap in our understanding of culture and society (Bruner 1991; Czarniawska 1999, 2000, 2004; Larsen 2002; Mumby 1993; Zelizer 1993). A culture involves working 'mentally' in common, writes Bruner, and one of the principal ways we do this is through the process of 'joint narrative accrual'. These narratives 'depend on being placed within a continuity provided by a constructed and shared social history in which we locate our Selves and our individual continuities' (Bruner 1991: 20).

Rather than producing sketchy accounts, often at high levels of abstraction, the study of narrative attunes the scholar to nuance, helping us see things that would be overlooked in more technical readings and absences as well as presences (Robertson 2000, 2002). Narrative encourages us to focus on human agency and is a valuable approach because it 'deals with the particular and the specific, rather than the collective and statistical' (Kiser 1996: 250).

It is rare to encounter a work on narrative that does not invoke *Morphology of the Folktale*, written by the Russian formalist Vladimir Propp in 1928. A classic example of structural analysis, the *Morphology* classified Slavic fairytales 'according to their component parts and their relationship to each other and to the whole' (Propp 1968: 19). After having analysed 100 tales, Propp was able to document a recurrence in storylines, characters (such as hero, villain, donor, helper) and what he referred to as 'functions', by which he meant both the actions of the characters and the consequences of these actions for the story. Propp claimed that, despite the vast number of folktales in circulation, there were not more than thirty-one functions (which ranged from 'initial situation', 'violation' and 'hero's reaction' to 'pursuit', 'rescue', 'recognition' and 'punishment'). While his conclusions are both exciting and compelling, the analysis itself is turgid, with Propp picking away at the stories until they are skeletons devoid of flesh and colour. A point is also missed if the focus is on the universality of these characters and functions rather than on the way they are deployed differently in different cultural settings. Nevertheless, narratology – i.e. an approach to the study of narratives that attends to their structures – was further developed after Propp by a diverse array of scholars, initially in the former Soviet Union and France and then beyond. Many narrativists continue to be heavily inspired by structuralism and tend to write as though narrative analysis was, quite simply, the analysis of the structure of stories (one example is Riessman). Others (such as Kiser) pit a narrative approach *against* a structuralist approach, for example to historical sociology.

Narrative is a concept that is also often associated with post-modernism. This is largely thanks to Lyotard, who argued that the 'postmodern condition' was one in which a few meta-narratives had been replaced by countless micro-narratives. He used the term 'narrative knowledge' to refer to ways of knowing that differ from monological conceptions of truth, which tended to be rational and scientific (Lyotard 1984: 18). For many, 'the narrative turn' in the social sciences was coterminous with the rise of postmodernism as an influential perspective; the notion of the 'narrative paradigm' was at any rate first invoked by Walter Fisher in 1984 (Mumby 1993: 2), the same year as Lyotard's *The Postmodern Condition* was published.

Despite this lineage, narrative analysis is not the preserve of structuralists or postmodernists. When it comes to theory, mod-ernists as prominent as Giddens have written of narrative. When it comes to practice, some empiricists have gone so far as to combine a narrative approach with theoretical frameworks involving the rational actor (Garme 2001; Kiser 1996), while others maintain that narratives can be used in research as a complement to tools familiar from quantitative research, such as experiments, observation and surveys (Lieblich et al. 1998: 1). The analyses in the chapters that follow occupy the middle ground between these ambitions.

If narrative analysis is to work as an analytical approach, it is necessary to define the object of analysis. At its most basic, a narrative is an account of something that has happened, be it in reality or in the imagination. A common definition of narrative, particularly among structuralists, has to do with its being the organization of events into a plot (Bremond [1966] 1980: 390; Kozloff 1992: 69–70; Somers 1994: 616).[2] Improving on and streamlining Propp's formalist model, Labov analysed narratives in terms of their formal properties and functions. He identified six common elements: an abstract (or summary of the narrative); an orientation (as to the time, place, situation and participants); a complicating action; an evaluation (involving the narrator's attitude; here the meaning of the action is commented on); a resolution (i.e. what finally happened); and a coda, which returns the perspective to the present (Labov and Waletsky 1967).

A key aspect of the definition of narrative has to do with its relation to discourse, in the sense of being that which is expressed in a given social context. Some, such as Barthes ([1966] 1977) and Bruner (1991), see it as *indistinguishable* from discourse. Others view narrative as a possible *form* of discourse – as one sort of text among many circulating in society (Mottier 1999). Riessman (1993: 17) considers it as something *detachable* from a surrounding discourse.

The definition of narrative put to work in the empirical studies that follow is derived from Labov and from Chatman (1978: 19), who defines narrative as something consisting of a story (or a 'what' – the events and orientation referred to by Labov) *and* a discourse (a 'how', with a focus on the way a story is communicated, and not just its structure). It is thus a form of discourse in the sense that the way the story is communicated is influenced by social practices and generic conventions. It contains some, but not necessarily all, of the elements and functions stipulated by structuralist theorists.

Fernsehen: looking at television

Insights into the preconditions for emergent cosmopolitan understandings and perhaps even identities – for 'seeing far' (as the

Germans chose to designate television) and for making connections with distant others – can be gained by looking not just at *what* is reported about the world, but also *how* it is reported. By attending to the narrative techniques used in reporting the world, and to the stories in which information about the events of the day is packaged, it is possible to see that it is not a flurry of disjointed sound bites and images that are flung in our faces every time we turn on the evening news. Rather, television news programmes can be seen to rehearse a number of recurrent themes, some of which are 'universal' (or at least common to different newsrooms), but some of which differ in intriguing ways, according to whether the narrator is a British journalist, for example, or a German or Swede, and whether he or she is addressing a global or European audience or a national one. This means that television is treated here as a site for community-enhancing storytelling.[3]

Interpretive frameworks 'of common, cultural references and thematic codes, incarnated in master or model narratives', help make things comprehensible and relevant to the public (Birkvad 2000: 295). In these, the cultural and the political intersect. Documenting them, and explaining how they work, presents a methodological challenge, but the effort can be worth it, as it can teach us much about cultural power in a globalized world. Unlike ideology, master narratives tend to be experienced as something innocent, because they are naturalized (Barthes 1993: 131). What a narrative approach attempts to gain analytical purchase on is the generation of these sorts of understandings – what is taken for granted, or that which goes without saying.

To grasp how these sorts of understandings appear natural while being so insidious and powerful, it is necessary to follow the advice of Szernszynski and Urry and look to convention. Illusions of verisimilitude, explains Brinker, are based on the viewer's 'thoroughgoing familiarity with the conventions of representation' at work (Brinker 1983: 254). Such conventions are routinely deployed by journalists, who can be seen, if not as mythologists, then at least as storytellers. Audiences recognize and interpret these conventions without even noticing it, through naturalization. As Chatman explains it, 'to naturalize a narrative convention means not only to understand it, but to "forget" its conventional character, to absorb it into the reading-out process', by which he means our routinely employed abilities to decode from surface to narrative structures (Chatman 1978: 41–2). Even young children, he explains, see a puff of smoke at the feet of a figure in a cartoon and know to decode it as indicating speed, or a bubble with small clouds leading from it to a figure's head as indicating thought. The illusion of reality and naturalness is secured by the complete familiarity of the viewer with the conventions of representation used in a given text, familiarity which Brinker tells us 'breeds an unawareness of the existence of these conventions' (Brinker 1983: 254).

In writing about how people relate to images, Aumont refers to an activity he dubs 'the etcetera law' (paraphrasing John F. Kennedy). 'The spectator, by virtue of his or her prior knowledge, makes up for what is lacking, that is to say, he or she supplies what is not represented in the image' (Aumont 1997: 60). The spectator, or viewer, can organize reality and 'match percepts with icons that have been previously encountered and are stored in schematic form in the memory', combining recognition and recall. The example of a report that appeared on one of the channels featured in this book some years before the period analysed can illustrate this possibility. Broadcast on the day they formally applied for membership, it was ostensibly about the desire of former Warsaw Pact states to join the European Union. However, as one group of insiders (French, German and Swedish experts in Brussels) were heard giving their views on the topic, another group of insiders (the television viewers for whom the report was intended, with the cultural resources to use the etcetera law) were treated to a striking medley of images which included peasants trudging through their fields behind horse-drawn ploughs, forests killed by the black smoke belching out of factory chimneys, and environmentally hostile East European automobiles. One of the images was particularly suitable for interpretation with reference to the etcetera law. When presented with a scene of a Gothic castle on a rockface, viewers presumably needed no additional information (and indeed were given none) than the shot of an adjacent signpost, which informed them that the edifice was Dracula's castle, to fill in the missing information. Activating recall of icons encountered in popular culture and stored in schematic form ('stranger', 'irredeemable', 'sinisterly threatening' or perhaps 'slightly comic'), it is easy to speculate on the sense that viewers would have made of political activity resulting in the incorporation of Romania (and hence also Transylvania) in the EU, by filling in the 'missing' scepticism.

This need not have been consciously done. To use Beck's terminology, the understandings that are tapped into with such heuristic devices are often latent. As consumers of television news, we rarely give a thought to camera angles, but routinely and sub-consciously decode the physical distance established by the filming and editing of a news story as associated with social distance. Media researchers (particularly in Anglo-Saxon countries) have noted how politicians tend to appear in news bulletins at a respectable distance, while ordinary people tend to be shown at closer quarters, particularly if they are in distress. This convention is thought to have the effect of putting the average viewer in a more intimate relation with the sort of figures with whom they are presumed to be on an equal social footing. Unreliable figures can be looked up at if the journalist's intention is to depict them as menacing, down on when they are to look less powerful, and filmed at an oblique angle when they are situated as 'other' (Graddol 1994: 142). There need be nothing sinister in this. Television news is no different from other genres when it comes to using technology, artifice and naturalized conventions of representation in general, even if the complaint lodged years ago by Graddol (ibid.: 137) that the visual element of news was undertheorized is still in the in-box.

Graddol identified two traditions used in television journalism to tell stories about the world. The dominant one is 'realism', a term originally used (except by international relations scholars) to refer to a literary convention. The narrator in this tradition tends to be omniscient – 'one who can see things which individual characters cannot see and who is in all places at once'. Other characters can also contribute to the narrative, but they are encompassed by the omniscient narrator's voice. The other tradition is that of 'naturalism'. Used more often in documentaries than in news bulletins, it provides 'a representation of the world as it might be directly experienced by the viewer. [. . .] From a naturalist perspective, a news report provides a vicarious experience, an image of the world as we might expect to experience it if we were to stand where the reporter stands.' The objective, omniscient narrator's voice is absent from reports in which naturalist narrative techniques are used (Graddol 1994: 140–5). Naturalism is considered a powerful ideological technique, which represents a subjective view on how actors are discursively related to each other and the world. The difference between realist and naturalist representation is akin to the difference between the 'panoptic controlling male gaze', through which difference and distance are confirmed, and the 'mobile' gaze that Nava characterizes as female and more conducive to a cosmopolitan outlook (Nava 2007: 25–6).

These are among the ideas that have inspired and informed the study presented in the pages that follow. But an attempt has been made to problematize Graddol's understanding of the way distance is achieved – and overcome – in television news reporting. Given the particular interest here in cosmopolitanization, the relationship constructed between the intended audience and the figures populating news stories is important. In Graddol's account, elites are empowered by being depicted at a distance, while ordinary people suffer the presumably opposite fate of being viewed at closer quarters. But if the concern is to locate news narratives in which audiences are encouraged to feel themselves at home in the world, and to identify with people from different places and with different fates from their own, then it is important to pay attention to the contexts in which 'ordinary people' are seen in close-up and when they are kept at arm's length, either by distance or by being depicted on the other side of a barrier from the viewer – behind a door or window or barbed wire fence, or behind a weapon such as that of the Sudanese fighter in plate 1.1.

Jameson and Lyotard are famous for the bleak view they take of contemporary mediascapes, which they see as characterized by disjointed information flows, trivialization and superficiality. Lyotard juxtaposes precapitalist cultures founded on narrative practices, in which repetition was incorporated 'as an integral part of their narrativity', with post-industrial capitalist society and its language games, to the detriment of the latter. For his part, Jameson insists that television lacks memory, historical depth, and thus narrative coherence (cited in Rowe 1994: 99).

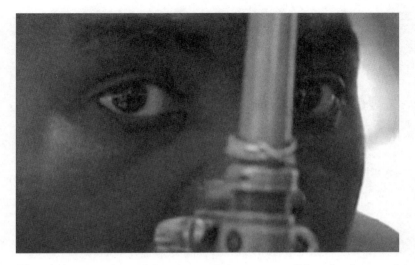

Plate 1.1   A Sudanese fighter seen in close-up, yet cut off from the viewer, and without a mouth to engage the viewer in dialogue

In this chapter, it has been suggested that it is an empirical question whether or not 'the media' are guilty of this. Television news in particular, often thought to overwhelm us with new information every day and, indeed, every hour, can be seen as a source, not of forgetting, but of recurrent narratives that keep cultural memories and shared understandings alive. As discussed earlier, however, the 'theory' of such narrative frameworks can be used to deal with new 'data' coming in from a global environment undergoing rapid change and becoming continually more complex. The next chapter considers some of the data that has been in circulation, and how discursive conventions used to relay it to European viewers may be thought to reinforce different theories or narrative structures. It is possible that such work may result in viewing that is sophisticated in the way Boulding had in mind.

2
Reporting the World Back to Itself: Comparing News Coverage to Domestic and Global Publics

It was suggested in the preface that journalists, at least in the public service broadcasting sector, are very much aware of the responsibility with which they are entrusted, not only to report the events of the day in a fair and accurate way, but also to make those events meaningful to the publics they serve. Such a sense of responsibility derives in part from their training or personal convictions (the sort of ethics that compel journalists to feel they have to report the world from many different perspectives in order to report the world back to itself). But it also derives from the mandate given journalists and media organizations by the political institutions that regulate them.

Governing authorities have set out clear guidelines for public service broadcasters operating in a national setting. Swedish Television, for example, has been assigned the role of a 'major player in developing a society of ethnic and cultural diversity'. Part of its mission is 'to counteract prejudice and stereotypical thinking as well as to increase people's awareness of one another and their understanding of persons from different ethnic and cultural backgrounds' (SVT 2006).

Policies and ambitions are one thing. In a competitive, commercial environment, however, when complicated events must be explained under severe time constraints to audiences with unclear levels of knowledge or engagement, the reality is often something different. Nor is it entirely clear what are the responsibilities of organizations that have their roots in a public service culture, but which service a public beyond the borders of the reporting nation. A press release issued by the BBC Press Office in October 2007 announced that elites rated BBC World as the leading news channel for impartiality, authority and relevance in the European Opinion Leaders survey. Unfortunately, neither the press release nor the survey explained the key term 'relevance'. Relevant to what and to whom? To the European business, government, media and academic elites who participated in the survey, obviously. But what about non-elite viewers? If, as the Al Jazeera advertisement mentioned at the end of the preface suggests, the task is to report the world back to itself, does this mean the world of cosmopolitan elites, or is there a responsibility to reflect the inhabitants of a wider global community, and their concerns, back to themselves and their counterparts?

As was set out in the first chapter, the power of community consists in 'the emergence of definitions, principles and cognitive methods for imagining the world'. Delanty (2003: 157) put it well when he said that the power of community is essentially the power of communication. In this chapter, it will be argued that the power of the news media in a globalized world involves not just the imparting of the accurate, impartial and reliable information so esteemed by opinion leaders and proponents of civic cosmopolitanism. The power of television news resides in its potential to engage its viewers, as well as to inform them, to help them to remember as well as to know, and to make it possible for them to recognize and identify with the distant Others who populate their televisions screens, rather than just to sit back and be a spectator. It will be argued, moreover, that, in order to explicate these different dimensions of power, it is necessary to use a combination of analytical techniques, both quantitative and interpretive. The question guiding the analysis presented below is: How *is* the world reported back to itself? Does reporting vary in significant ways depending on the news culture in question? Are different sorts of audiences (national as opposed to global, for example, or Britons as opposed to Swedes) told different sorts of stories about their political, social and cultural environment?

The focus of this chapter, then, is on television news narratives and their potential power to engage rather than to inform. It will be argued that this power can be performed in different ways, to different degrees, or on different dimensions. The first has to do with the promotion of *awareness*. What is happening in the world and where? To whom is it happening? Here, it could be argued, is the locus of what Beck (2006) refers to as 'latent cosmopolitanism'.

The second involves the activation of that which concerns both Boltanski and Chouliaraki – the appeal to pity, or at least to sympathy. But the people I feel sorry for may not necessarily be like me; they may not belong in my world. A distinction should be made between engagement in this dimension and a third sort, which is possible in a Meyrowitzian 'placeless' world. When news narratives invite identification, the viewer is encouraged to imagine that the distant other is not distant at all. The journalist may bring us to the Other, or bring the Other to us, or otherwise urge us to consider that 'this could be *me*'. It is here that what Beck identifies as a constitutive principle of cosmopolitanism comes into play: the principle of 'perspective-taking' – the capacity and willingness to put oneself in the position of the other.

Different newsrooms, different windows on the world

Three of the newsrooms whose output was analysed are publicly financed broadcasters with a mandate to service national audiences, in the UK, Germany and Sweden. Two are channels which broadcast advertisements but which have roots in the public service tradition, targeting audiences outside the reporting country, which were in this case the UK and Germany. The sixth and final channel has to be labelled 'European', quite simply.[1]

Attention must be paid to how media actors work 'in concert' with political and social institutions. The three national broadcasters featured in this chapter, together with the additional two included in the study reported in chapter 4, represent each of the three models of media and politics identified by Hallin and Mancini (2004). Sweden and Germany conform to the 'democratic corporatist' model, characterized by a high level of journalistic professionalization, including a commitment to what is thought to be a common public interest, and autonomy from other social powers. Both countries have a strong tradition of public service broadcasting, and the two channels in the sample have held their own despite competition in recent decades from commercial new-comers. The Swedish programmes analysed here were broadcast at 7.30 p.m. by SVT. An institution since 1969 and the largest news programme in the country, *Rapport* serves 9 million Swedes with 30 minutes of news at that time each day. The German program, *Heute*, is slightly shorter (20 minutes) and airs at 7 p.m. For forty years it has been the main newscast of Germany's second channel, ZDF, and, with 13 per cent of the share of the 82 million-strong German audience, lags just slightly behind the first channel. Despite the differences in the absolute number of viewers, *Rapport* and *Heute* share a similar culture when it comes to the political role of the media.

Britain represents the 'liberal' or 'Anglo-American' model of media and politics. This entails a professional ethos centred on the principle of objectivity (Hallin and Mancini 2004: 227). It shares with the democratic corporatists a strong tradition of public service broadcasting, of which the BBC is indeed the prototype. The *Ten O'Clock News*, considered here, is the BBC's news flagship. The 30-minute programme is watched by more Britons daily (4.9 million viewers per night, on average) than any other.[2]

The three other channels whose output is analysed in this chapter are global in reach and target audience, but not in origin and moor-ings. BBC World, one of the world's oldest global broadcasters, has an audience of over 230 million people weekly – more than its leading competitor, CNN. Under the remit of the state-funded World Service, it is also dependent on commercial revenues. The 30-minute news programme that is broadcast daily at 10 p.m. CET is the basis for this analysis. Deutsche Welle is also partially funded by advertisements, but owned by the German state. It has broadcast internationally and in Germany since 1953 and has been available on television since 1992. EuroNews, launched in 1993, is the

Table 2.1 Material on which chapter 2 is based: the main evening news broadcast by the BBC (UK domestic), ZDF (German domestic), SVT (Swedish domestic), BBC World (UK-based global), Deutsche Welle (German-based global) and EuroNews (Europe-based global), 26 April–13 June 2004

	BBC	*Heute*	*Rapport*	BBC World	Deutsche Welle	Euro-News	Total
No. of programmes	40	49	49	49	49	49	285
Minutes coded	925	844	1182	1346	1159	741	6197
Average mins/day	23	17	24	27	24	15	130
No. items coded	420	610	705	548	571	536	3390
Average no. items/day	10.5	12.4	14.4	11	11.6	11	11.8

youngest of the channels in the sample. Broadcasting in a variety of languages to 193 million households in 121 countries (although actually watched in considerably fewer), it is funded partly by the European Commission and the European Broadcasting Union and partly by advertisements. It broadcasts without an anchor or, for the most part, visible reporters, and its news bulletin (the length of which can be difficult to ascertain, but is about 30 minutes on average) tends to be telegraphic in reporting style.

The study reported in this chapter involved the analysis of slightly more than 100 hours of news – the contents of 285 daily news bulletins, broadcast over a period of seven weeks in 2004 (see table 2.1). It began with the countdown to the enlargement of 1 May, when former Eastern bloc countries joined the European Union. For viewers not interested in politics, there was the possibility of interacting with other Europeans in the popular public sphere with the staging of the Eurovision Song Contest, the kick-off to the Euro 2004 football championships and a couple of royal weddings, all broadcast live to foster communal mediated experiences. Outside Europe there were floods in the Caribbean, an earthquake in Iran, a brewing genocide in the Sudan and disclosures of US army-perpetrated torture in Iraq's Abu Ghraib prison to engage the sympathies of television viewers with distant others.

As every scholar knows, it is important to analyse primary source material with care, to re-examine it and to reinterpret it time and again. The media researcher has an obligation on top of that to bear in mind that the people for whom the material was originally intended generally view it only once, and seldom with their full attention. Mindful that television is a flow, each broadcast was first viewed in its entirety and impressions documented of the world upon which each newsroom opened a window. After each broadcast had been watched, a brief answer was noted at the bottom of the codesheet to the question: How does the world I live in look through the window provided by this television screen today?

The world of the BBC *Ten O'Clock News* in this period was one characterized by war, terror and threats to the world economy emanating from Islamic fundamentalism. It tended to be seen from the perspective of elites and others charged with protecting security within and outside the UK. EU enlargement had much to do with security, law enforcement and illegal immigration (as well as the usual bureaucracy).

The world refracted through the lens of Germany's *Heute* also contained military conflict, but so much attention was paid to economic affairs that it seemed characterized equally by cooperation. While ordinary people could be seen and heard in domestic settings, the international environment was populated largely by elites and abstractions: this viewer was left without an impression of ever getting close to other people in the outside world. On the BBC, journalists such as Clive Myrie, pictured in plate 2.1, were the only ones to explain complicated issues in a pedagogical way. On the German news, academics and other experts were used in this capacity. This is a feature *Heute* shared with its Swedish counterpart, *Rapport*.

While BBC reporters talked *down* to viewers and German reporters talked *to* them, Swedish reporters seemed to position themselves *beside* viewers and quite often asked the same sort of (often 'stupid') questions an ordinary person might have posed. The Swedish world also resembled *Heute*'s in being characterized by cooperation as well as conflict. It was a world in which domestic affairs (some of them remarkably parochial) were of apparent importance, but also one in which an exciting new Europe was

Plate 2.1　The pedagogical BBC reporter teaches viewers about 'forgotten wars'

on the doorstep: the strains of Beethoven's *Ode to Joy* provided the metaphorical soundtrack to the Swedish programme, even when out of tune or played in the wrong key.

In BBC World, on the other hand, as on the domestic BBC channel, it was the rumble of artillery and blasts of exploding cars in Iraq that could be heard continually in the background. The World News was populated by political and military leaders, and the primary definers tended to be men. Not only was this a world dominated by armed conflict: by the end of the sample period – when the sixtieth anniversary of D-Day coincided with the death of Ronald Reagan – it was easy to get the impression that some wars, and the warriors waging them, were being glorified.

Deutsche Welle flagged itself as being 'at the heart of Europe', and it appeared that the slogan was not taken lightly. Like the Swedish programme, DW made use of non-journalists as experts in debriefings (notably academics). It often adopted an elite perspective (there were many government leaders, heads of state and soldiers populating these broadcasts), but it differed in interesting ways from the other programmes in terms of the countries and events covered. While commemorating war, like the two British broadcasters, it also observed the tenth anniversary of South

African democracy and of the Chernobyl accident, and in general gave significant coverage to environmental concerns. Most attention was paid to the economy, however, which meant that the overarching impression gained from routine viewing of this programme was of a world characterized by cooperation, and not just conflict. While making news for different sorts of audiences, then, the newsrooms based in the same country (the two BBCs and the two German programmes, respectively) resembled each other in ways that matter to this study.

EuroNews, finally, proved frustratingly difficult to code, despite the apparent simplicity of most of its items. Reporters were seldom seen in the main body of the newscast: reports were, with few exceptions, voiceovers built on news agency footage. Given the source of the material, a lot of space tended to be offered to official government and EU sources, and the tone of reporting seemed to be telegraphic and distanced. For precisely these reasons, it is interesting to see how different the EuroNews agenda could be from that of broadcasters such as the BBC. Leaders could be seen here that were rarely, if ever, glimpsed elsewhere (EU, Italian, Spanish and French leaders). Compared with the BBC programmes, there was a distinct lack of respect for US President Bush, and the emphasis in reports of the Iraq conflict was more on the jubilation with which returning troops were greeted than words of praise for the brave men fighting for democracy and freedom in the Middle East. Space was given to dissenting voices not only in reporting on Iraq but also − interestingly − in EU coverage. Civil society was very much in evidence in the world of EuroNews.

The first impressions given by these 285 newscasts suggest that claims about the homogenization of news in the global media era, to the extent that they continue to be bandied about, are problematic. The world does not look the same when viewed through different televisions screens, even if many of the images flickering across those screens are the same. They are incorporated in different ways into different stories about the international environment.

Given that cosmopolitanism has to do with an ability and readiness to engage with people and cultures beyond the borders of the nation, and with the widening of consciousness, a very basic starting point for the analysis was to ask how much scope the different broadcasts gave for such engagement by opening a 'window on the world'. How much of the world of each broadcast was taken up by parochial concerns, and how often was the viewer's attention drawn to what was happening beyond the borders of the reporting country?

Each news item in the sample was coded as to whether it was purely a domestic item,[3] a news item in which the reporting country intersected with the outside world, or an item that dealt solely with events in the outside world, without any connection to the reporting country.

One broadcaster stands out in the results of this categorization: BBC World. It is in a class of its own when it comes to the proportion of its contents that have to do with the world beyond the UK. At the other end of the scale, the Swedish programme is that which devotes most attention, when measured in terms of the number of news items, to purely domestic affairs. The finding that the coverage of the domestic BBC programme is reasonably evenly balanced in terms of domestic and foreign focus can be attributed largely to Britain's involvement in, and preoccupation with, the war in Iraq. Nevertheless, it would seem that the Swedish newsroom has the most parochial output of the six, and BBC World would seem to offer the cosmopolitan viewer the best news diet. Of the three broadcasters producing news for national audiences, this preliminary overview also indicates that the BBC tells its viewers more often than the Germans and Swedes that the concerns of the outside world are also the concerns of Britons (i.e. it scores highest on the proportion of 'intersecting' news items).

A study of how television news reporting could be thought to contribute to, or work against, the development of a cosmopolitan consciousness on the part of its viewers could obviously not end here, however. A more interpretive analysis of the news reports that were a minute or more in length indicated that the results presented in figure 2.1 need to be problematized.

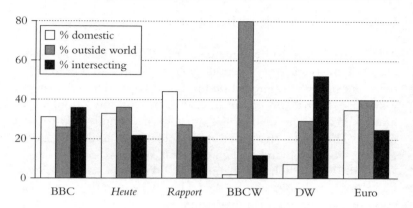

Figure 2.1 Distribution of news in the 285 broadcasts, seen in terms of spatial location.

Beyond awareness: two more compelling levels of engagement

As explained in chapter 1, the primary concern of this analysis was to explore whether the news was presented in such a way as to suggest it may have had something to do with the average viewer. Were news stories told in a way in which people could be thought to relate to them? If news reports engage viewers, as well as inform them about the world beyond their doorstep, and help them to identify with, or at least understand and not just observe, distant others, then it is reasonable to say that they could be thought to contribute to Beck's emergent 'cosmopolitan outlook'. Paying attention to how relationships between the people populating news broadcasts and those watching them are shaped by journalistic storytelling techniques – for example, whether they are in the realist or naturalist tradition – is one way of exploring this. Three sets of reports, relating similar or identical events, broadcast on channels targeting different national audiences, can serve as illustrations.

Upstairs downstairs: a British story of the new Europe

A few days before EU enlargement, the BBC *Ten O'Clock News* reported 'the tragic story' of an illegal immigrant found dead in the basement of the prestigious London Café Royal. The 47-year-old Ukrainian, a qualified engineer, had been working a double 12-hour shift when he died in the squat he had improvised to save money. The story is structured around the theme of divides – geographic, economic and metaphorical. It opens where he began, and with the family he left behind: 'In Ukraine, a widow grieves, mourning for a husband who died a lonely death a thousand miles away in London, for a family shattered.'

Viewers are told how Roman Kobitovich, a devoted father, could not make enough money in his native Ukraine to give his daughters a university education. For their sake, he travelled illegally to Britain to find work. The widow lays out a meal in her tiny home in Western Ukraine, as we look down on her daughters sitting over their economics and medical textbooks. Without their father, we are told, they will have little chance of finishing the courses that cost £1,000 a year. For most of Ukraine's 50 million people, life has been tough since the collapse of the Soviet Union: a third live in poverty. Thousands have left to look for work in Europe. The poor little Ukrainian home and a street with beggars are contrasted in the next shot with the opulence of the Café Royal – the London establishment in which Roman worked above stairs and lived below. The meaning of the story is commented on by the reporter in what would be referred to as the 'resolution' in narrative analysis. '"We weren't happy about him going abroad", says Natalia, "but there wasn't any other way." And that is the tragedy of Roman Kobitovich's death: a loving father who wanted the best for his daughters, enough to travel illegally to Britain to help them, but whose journey to London has only left his family worse off than before.'

This item, I would argue, works at the second level of engagement. It promotes awareness ('the lonely death of a restaurant cleaner has shed new light on the lives of London's half a million immigrant workers') and goes a step further, telling Roman Kobitovich's story in a way that invites our sympathy. It is not difficult to argue that the average viewer would be inclined to feel sorry for Roman and his family. Although the reporter uses personification techniques, the message is that the dead cleaner is typical: 'There's a whole generation of Roman Kobitoviches, decent, educated men struggling to get by', the reporter informs us in this closed text. But the narrative techniques at work in the story keep us at a distance from him and his plight, rather than encouraging us to go a step further and identify with him. We overhear Roman's widow and daughter speaking to the reporter, but they neither look at us nor speak to us directly. The reporter enters their home, but we are somehow left standing in the doorway, looking on. I would also argue that the resolution works to distance us from the illegal workers. The message is that people from poor countries will end up worse off if they try to make the class trip to the affluent West. It's tragic, the journalist seems to be saying, but apparently a fact of life. This is not the sort of message that invites us to take action, other than to sigh and shake our heads.

Building bridges: a Swedish story of the new Europe

Architectural metaphors recur in other narratives in the sample. While the story of the basement death of the Ukrainian cleaner juxtaposed the 'upstairs' with the 'downstairs' of the international class society and cast it in personal rather than political terms, the EU expansion of 1 May provided a political context for numerous items structured around the metaphors of walls torn down and bridges crossed. An item typical of Swedish television news discourse was broadcast a few days after the BBC aired its tragic account. The Swedish story had as its point of departure the town of Nova Gorica, on the border between Slovenia and Italy.

The story opens with a shot of a police van driving past a barrier and disappearing into the distance. The reporter, who is heard but never seen, makes the message of this text clear from the outset: 'Conflicts build walls between people, and friends and families are divided. After the Second World War, the border was redrawn here in the area. Old Gorica remained on the Italian side. On the Yugoslavian side, the town was renamed New Gorica. On May

Plate 2.2   East meets West on Swedish Television's Rapport *as the Kuscer family leave the old bloc and meet their Italian friends in the new Europe*

1st 2004 the map has been redrawn once again.' A family walks towards the camera (a contrast to the retreating police vehicle), passing a sign with the word 'Slovenia' surrounded by golden EU stars. This, the reporter tells us, as the angle changes and we find ourselves following them over the border, is the Kuscer family, who are celebrating the historic event by visiting their Italian friends (see plate 2.2).

Just a few years after independence from Yugoslavia, Slovenia has now chosen to relinquish some of its sovereignty and join the EU, we are told, as we see the Italian and Slovenian families meet, laugh and shake hands. The camera rests on the children of the two families, sitting side by side now that the Kuscers have entered the Italian home. Igor Kuscer tells us (in his own words, rather than being paraphrased by the reporter): 'Above all I expect that the children will become equal in Europe. Slovenia has been outside Europe for eighty years. During that time our children have been seen as worth less. Now I hope they can be equal. That they can go to school in Italy or Sweden.' His wife adds that she looks forward to making new ties with Europe and exchanging experiences. She says she thinks it's going be 'really good'. In a brief complicating action, the reporter acknowledges that not everyone in Slovenia shares the Kuscers' views, but then swiftly goes on to say that a large majority consider EU membership to have considerable advantages. These are not primarily economic ones. 'For Slovenians, membership is about historic and emotional ties to Europe', says the reporter, commenting on the meaning of all this in the resolution of the narrative. 'And the EU is a guarantee that they won't end up behind a new Iron Curtain.'

India – exotic and strange: a British story

'It's the world's biggest democratic exercise and the polls have now closed on the final day of India's general election', began the BBC newsreader on 10 May 2004. He went on to explain that India's Muslim minority was worried that the country's secular constitution would be threatened if the Hindu Nationalist Party was returned to power. The reporter in India took over at this point, speaking to us from the banks of a busy river. He stands between us and the people bathing and praying in it, most strikingly a man with a white beard, bare torso, loincloth and white mark on his forehead, sitting cross-legged and reading from what seems to be a holy book (see plate 2.3).

Filthy and germ-ridden though these waters may be, says the reporter, they are 'believed by these pilgrims to have cleansing powers'. More than 80 per cent of the Indian people are Hindus, and the government would like to 'give the country more of a saffron hue'. Another election victory would strengthen calls from hardliners to pursue a Hindu agenda that opponents and critics claim would deliberately discriminate against Muslims, we are told.

The scene shifts to archive footage of Hindu protesters tearing down a sixteenth-century mosque, then cuts to a shot of masons hammering and chiselling stone to be used in the temple they are building in its place. There is then a close-up of a man chanting into a microphone. This, explains the reporter, 'is the authentic

Plate 2.3   India on the eve of the election

voice of Hindu fundamentalism: the activists who took part in the destruction of the mosque. We'll tear down more, he cries, and build more temples.' Another cut shows us the city of Mumbai which, viewers are told, is not just India's financial hub, but the scene of the worst communal violence in the wake of the mosque's destruction, in which 900 people were killed. The report ends with a view of a sea of men on prayer mats with their heads on their knees, and the reporter's pronouncement: 'It is the fear of Muslims that a BJP victory could usher in a more destructive doctrine.'

India – oddly familiar: a Swedish story

Meanwhile, in the *Rapport* newsroom, the Swedish newsreader was telling her viewers that the world's biggest democratic election was coming to a close and that the outcome was uncertain, as neither the government nor the opposition looked likely to win a majority. The report began not in a dirty holy river, but at a polling station. As in many reports of Swedish elections, which feature empty rooms with ballots, the invisible reporter told viewers that the 650 million Indians eligible to vote had not exactly rushed to the polls. 'Voting turnout could well be far below 50 per cent – a clear indication that people are not satisfied with the options.'

An Indian man, speaking English and identified as a political analyst, is seen in close-up as he explains that people are faced with a choice between 'reposing confidence in an ageing, ailing prime minister [. . .] and a foreign-born, incoherent, not at all dynamic woman leader'. The reporter picks up on the theme of electoral apathy and explains that it came as a surprise to the governing coalition, as the country was doing so well. To shots of happy, well-dressed families going up escalators in shopping malls and young Indians in Western clothes going in and out of smart-looking shops, his voice can be heard saying: 'Peace overtures with Pakistan, rapid economic growth – almost 10 per cent this year – and an increasingly prosperous middle class: some 150 million Indians can afford to shop at Western-inspired shopping centres like this.'

The reporter then takes us into a family home, and we see a tea tray being set down in front of us. 'We go to visit Kiran Misra,' the still invisible reporter says, 'a typical representative of the Indian middle class, as she herself says.' We find ourselves face to face with Kiran (see plate 2.4), whose fluent English is subtitled in Swedish, allowing her to speak directly to the viewer about things they can relate to: 'If I were to compare it to what it was just ten years back, there's been a rapid development. Employment opportunities are now here like never before. So many foreign companies have been allowed to come in. And now there's this thing of independent entrepreneurship . . .'

But, the reporter points out in the complicating action of the narrative, most people are much poorer. The camera cuts to labourers digging ditches and harvesting tea. A man in a turban says (not in English this time) that he doesn't get paid regularly: the money comes when it comes. The reporter explains that the man, called Ram, cannot vote because his name is not on the register, and that, even if they were eligible, there is a problem because Ram's wife would only vote as her husband instructed. 'The poor', says the reporter, 'are smart enough to see that there is a big difference between their own and their politicians' lives.' Ram underlines this, so we understand why it doesn't really matter to him whether or not he gets to vote: 'It's the greedy who have

Det finns fler arbetstillfällen än nansin.

Plate 2.4   Kiran Misra talks about developments in the Indian economy, as well as their impact on the lives of the Indian middle class

power now. They grab as much money as they can and don't do anything else.' As the story ends, the reporter can finally be seen, standing at the corner of a busy street scene. The election, he concludes, could result in a long period of political instability, but also an end to the positive developments India had been experiencing economically, socially, politically and in foreign affairs. The story closes with a shot of people going down a city street.

Comparing stories

The British and Swedish television news stories about divisions between East and West can serve to illustrate the potential power of television to engage as well as to inform, but also how narrative techniques can encourage different sorts of engagement. Apart from making viewers aware of the world around them, a second order of narrative can involve the activation of pity or sympathy. But, as mentioned earlier, the people I feel sorry for – people such as the admirable Roman Kobitovich – may not necessarily be like me; they may not belong in the world in which I feel at home. The second narrative gives us cause to consider whether a distinction should be made between 'sympathetic' engagement and engagement built on identification. In reports such as those depicting political processes using personification techniques involving the Kuscer family and friends, the viewer is encouraged to imagine that the distant other is not distant at all. Here it is possible to observe Beck's 'perspective-taking' at work. When the Kuscers take us with them over the border into a new political community, and the invisible reporter points out that they have willingly surrendered some of their new-found independence to forge new ties with other countries, viewers are given the sort of semiotic material that can be used to imagine our situations as being interchangeable. Rather than standing awkwardly in the doorway, looking on at someone's suffering, audience members are given the capacity, at least discursively, to put themselves in the position of the other.

The message in the sympathetic but pessimistic BBC item is, it could be argued, that divisions will always be there and people, however good their intentions, can expect to continue living in a world characterized not least by an economic divide. The message in its Swedish counterpart, which is optimistic and arguably promotes identification with non-Swedes, is that divisions are contingent. Conflicts can end, walls can be scaled and bridges crossed when the political will exists. What is interesting here is that the desire to forge new relationships is depicted as the concern of ordinary people.

Differences in depictions of ordinary people are striking in the Indian stories too. From the newsreader's first sentence, the Indian election is framed in the BBC narrative as having to do with tensions between religious groups, a theme that resonates with other reporting in the sample (notably the bloodshed in Iraq and between Israel and the Palestinians). This overture could conceivably distance the British viewer immediately (unless, of course, he or she is one of the many of Asian descent), a narrative move that is reinforced by the opening scene of people bathing in a dirty river, clothed and behaving exotically. The reporter places himself between the viewer and the people in the story and

Plate 2.5   The 'realist' BBC narrator positions himself between the viewer and the distant others

never surrenders the position: he keeps us at a safe distance from the militants destroying an ancient place of worship and activists speaking strange tongues and chanting messages of racial hatred (see plate 2.5). In India, the viewer learns from this report, people bathe in filthy waters, build temples, and kill each other over religion. Indians are religious fundamentalists and speak strange languages – and speak to the reporter, not to us. The 'preferred reading' is apparently that the Indian election could result in further destruction.

In the Swedish narrative, it could be argued, the Indian election is a much more familiar event. In this version of India, people do the same thing as Swedes and other Europeans: they vote. Or they refrain from voting because they are cynical about the intentions of power-hungry politicians. Indians speak directly to us, in a language Swedes understand. They go shopping in the same sort of malls as Swedes, have a middle class that is educated and prosperous, like Sweden, and, at the side of the invisible reporter, we are invited into their homes to talk about the employment situation. India, in this account, is both different from Sweden (there are more people, only some of whom are dressed in Western clothes, and more traffic) and familiar (it has the same political system and problems, and people have the same concerns and react to them in familiar ways). It is easier to imagine sharing a world with SVT Indians than with BBC Indians, at least on the basis of these two reports.

Hannerz has suggested that cosmopolitanism can have a narcissistic streak, in that the self is constructed in the space where cultures mirror one another. When the viewer, in this analogy, encounters the other through the looking glass, understandings are expanded: 'a little more of the world is somehow under control' (1990: 240). In the examples shown here, the reporter could be said to play the role of the self, insofar as he is a representative of the viewer, from the same culture, standing in for him or her and lending his eyes and other senses and sharing his experiences. But in the two reporting cultures these 'selves' are differently constructed through different narrative techniques. When the self is constructed with recourse to realist narrative techniques, he is a spectator, looking on at the grief of a Ukrainian widow or the Indian bathing in filth. The world is somehow under control, but not in the way intended by Hannerz. Rather, it is under control because the viewer is protected from it by the knowledgeable correspondent who keeps it at arm's length. When the self is constructed with recourse to naturalist techniques, the reporter, and more importantly the viewer, becomes a participant – by walking beside a new European or drinking tea with an Indian school-teacher. A little more of the world has come under control because it has become a bit more familiar. Hannerz was referring to physical travel when he wrote that being on the move is not enough to turn people into cosmopolitans, but if we resort to analogy and think also in terms of armchair travellers, as Szerszynski and Urry do, the point he was making can be applied to the sort of competence encouraged by different narrative traditions. Tourists, as Hannerz reminded us, are not participants; tourism is largely a spectator sport (ibid.: 242).

3

The Woman with the Samsonite Suitcase: Journalists, Viewers, and Imagining How it is to be the Other

According to Brennan, the word 'cosmopolitan' captures the image intellectuals have of themselves. It has, in his account, to do with the proper way of being an intellectual, with thinkers seeking to understand difference by projecting outside themselves, while unconsciously 'translating' that alterity into local terms (Brennan 2002: 666–7). This is not an unusual understanding of the term. It is not just an assumption of political theory but a matter of 'common knowledge' that cosmopolitans are to be found at international academic conferences or at the airport business–class check-in counter. When writing this book, however, I have been interested in exploring whether cosmopolitans can also be found behind the wheel of a tractor or the desk of the local library. Is there any way of gaining empirical purchase on Beck's conviction that, under conditions of globalization, people are becoming cosmopolitans by default?

The examples of Swedish news narratives that featured in chapter 2 established the presence of naturalist conventions, with reporters off-screen privileging the accounts of the 'ordinary' people involved in the events they related. An issue to be addressed is whether such findings are evidence of conscious or unconscious behaviour. One purpose of this chapter is thus to pursue this lead one step further, by examining narratives on a particular topic – Sweden's 'near abroad' – and by talking to the journalists whose responsibility it was to put together these stories.

A second issue is whether or not such narratives, and the conventions used in the telling of such stories about the outside world, leave any impression on the sort of people for whom they are intended. The second purpose of this chapter is consequently to report the results of a foray into the 'field' – into the world of the living room – to talk to 'ordinary' people from the same media culture as the journalists about their relationship to the outside world and to the news that opens a window on it. As discussed in chapter 1, it is Appadurai's view that imagination has become social practice and the key component of the new global order. Mediascapes – such as those encountered in chapter 2 – offer repertoires of images and narratives that can be used in making sense of our lives and those of others. Given the focus of this book on interpretive frameworks of common cultural references and thematic codes, and its interest in workers of the imagination and not just their work, insights into the generation of understandings have been sought by talking to the senders and receivers of messages about the world beyond the borders of the nation, as well as to the stories encoded in those messages.

Rewinding the tape to the week before the EU opened its doors to former Soviet bloc states on 1 May 2004, this chapter listens to what one set of workers of the imagination had to say about what they had in mind when making news reports about this event and, more importantly, how they said it. In other words, this chapter presents a different sort of narrative than that so far encountered.

Journalists: taking a bit of the world into your living room

It is important, said the deputy head of Swedish Television's foreign news desk a few hours before flying to Poland to cover the World Economic Summit and EU accession, to highlight positive things in bringing news about the outside world to the Swedish public, and not just to problematize: 'you shouldn't confirm people's views.

You should continually change the perspective and in that way arouse more interest.' One way of doing that is to take the perspective of the average viewer, she said. Vox pops (interviews with 'the man on the street') are important, as the issues to which they refer have consequences for ordinary people. It is even better if the reporter gets to 'come in' somewhere.

SVT was devoting extra coverage to the new member states on the eve of enlargement, which was deemed important, given the widespread Euroscepticism in Sweden. 'We want to bring out other aspects,' said the deputy head, 'get people to meet on an equal level. We are not better than they are.' In her view, globalization in general and Europeanization in particular entail thinking along different lines than before: 'I think it is extremely important to understand that we are part of Europe. We are still our little edge of the world.'

A man who had worked at SVT for twenty-five years, with periods at the home news desk interspersed with stints covering Latin America, the US and Asia, spoke of the knack of 'seeing the world with Swedish eyes'. He thought it made a difference if viewers saw him rather than an American reporter standing on a rooftop in a distant city – taking a bit of the outside world and putting it into your living room, as he put it. 'Because I'm Swedish', he said, 'I have the same frame of reference' as the viewers in the aforementioned living room. This feeling of identification was, in his view, extremely important. In this respect, Swedish journalists tend to work differently from their colleagues in other countries. This correspondent had been to many places, he noted, where he was the only reporter who had gone up to people and talked to them: 'Being around ordinary people is important. You mustn't raise your voice.' He tried to get viewers to pay attention by pointing to 'the black woman in the shanty town of Soweto who is like you'. When he was asked how this strategy is to be understood – this strategy of speaking *to* ordinary people, not over their heads – the term 'dumbing down' cropped up. The journalist responded forcefully: the strategy he had been describing was absolutely *not* a question of that: 'What happens is something else. You find a red thread and hold onto it. You don't leave the viewer with seventeen unanswered questions after the report is finished. You don't confuse: you give them something.' You had to give the viewer an experience, he said. There is so much you want to tell, and the reporter has to do it in his or her own style. This man's style was 'shoulders down', relaxed, to enable people to keep up. 'It shouldn't feel like breaking news', he said.

Another man on the foreign news desk, who was SVT's Moscow correspondent between 1998 and 2002, was responsible for putting together the foreign news telegrams in the week before enlargement. He thought the extensive focus on the new EU members was a good strategy: 'It's a good technique to let the viewers meet their new neighbours. I think it's fun with lots of new countries.' The most important task a journalist has, in this respect, is to 'acquaint the viewers with the new countries. We have created a consciousness that Slovakia is a neighbour and just as good a country as ours.'

Having said that, 'we can never create belonging. We can't teach people how to live.' Adult education is a lovely idea, 'but who has given me the right to tell people how to think?'

For this journalist, the key word is 'meeting'. A good meeting between him and someone he encounters in the field can be seen as a meeting between 'the (wo)man in the field' and 'the (wo)man on the couch'. 'I'm not the star. It's the old man on the Russian ski slope and the woman in the Coptic village', he said, referring to people far from the halls of power on whom he had filed reports. When asked of a tendency observed in Swedish television news reports (Robertson 2000, 2002) to bring the viewer (metaphorically) into someone's home or the café they frequent, this journalist explained that it is a typical attitude among Swedish journalists. 'We want to be offstage, like an invisible choir.' They still have a role to play, however, even if they are not centre stage: namely that of a figure to whom the viewer can relate. 'They want to see themselves', he said, referring to the people watching *Rapport*. They want to see something that symbolizes common sense and coffee in the midst of chaos that is incomprehensible: 'When we see starving children with flies on their faces, we distance ourselves. When we see a Swede brush the flies away we notice, we say, "Oh, look – there are flies".'

One of the younger reporters on the foreign desk recalled

following reporting on the war in Kosovo, and how it took two or three months before reporting 'took hold' of her. Then one day she saw a picture of a woman carrying a Samsonite suitcase, with her daughter, dressed like any teenager familiar from a Stockholm setting. 'Then I realized: "Help! This could happen to me!"' What bothered her was the likelihood that there were a lot more Samsonite suitcases where that one came from. 'We are terrified of the modern', she said. 'We don't think it has to do with us unless we see pictures of a starving African child.'

Asked who or what she had in mind when putting together a story, she replied that she thought a lot about her father, who had a general, but not specialized, interest in the news. It is, she said, important to provide him and viewers like him with a 'context so that it becomes comprehensible'.

When it came to coverage of Europe, and especially enlargement, this journalist thought the heightened emphasis on reporting from the new member states to be a good idea, as it was important to 'reduce the distance between us and them'. Was it not editorializing, taking sides in favour of enlargement (as the director general of the BBC World Service suggested),[1] telling people they should admire Slovenians and Poles? She thought about this for a moment before replying that, 'as a journalist, you always take a stance'. This was not a matter of just relaying information: 'It should engage. Journalism means pointing at unsatisfactory conditions. A journalist should be the voice of the weak.' A journalist should 'widen the viewer's horizons', let the (wo)man on the couch know that 'this is how these people live, this is how they think'. Television is a powerful medium and such images are, in her view, important.

What is the result, the purpose of this? What are people supposed to do with these images, reports, messages and challenges? This sort of work, in the eyes of this journalist, should contribute to making 'a citizen who thinks more democratically with more respect for others'.

Finally, a senior reporter who had been covering Europe since 1996 expressed the decided view that many political journalists working the domestic beat made their reports for politicians and other political journalists rather than the licence-paying viewers. These political journalists do not have to make an effort to explain things, she said: they can use code words and ignore the need for pictures. This was not the case if you shifted the perspective on to what takes place outside the country. The task, as this woman identified it, was to make that which takes place abroad comprehensible to people in all parts of the country – in a little town in the north or in rural areas as well as in the capital – and with different levels of knowledge.

> You have to make it understandable. You have to explain it in a way that arouses the interest of the average guy and enables him to understand it straight away [. . .] You have to make your story fun and interesting – you have to tell your story in an exciting way so it stays with them [. . .] You can't expect everyone to recognize themselves. But you can use ordinary people that you can feel identification with, that you can relate to.

It is from the perspective of these 'ordinary' people out in the world that events must be depicted 'because, if people feel that "if this happened to them", they can draw the conclusion that "it can happen to me too".'

> We think that we in Sweden are so much better, have a better society than others. But we are just like everybody else in the whole world. We get up in the morning, go to work, deal with traffic and so on, and so do they. We face the same everyday problems. There are greater similarities than differences that we can exploit when we make television programmes.

In this way, this journalist believes 'we can create identification'. She said she hoped the viewer would react by thinking, 'Hey, I recognize this'.

Summary: the narrative of the newsroom

The interviews with these journalists contain many stories – about turning over a new leaf at the beginning of a career as European correspondent; about trying to get the home desk in Stockholm interested in German news; about interviewing an old man in the Carpathians; about 'the woman with the Samsonite suitcase'; and others. But, for the purposes of this discussion, it is more pertinent to reflect on the discourse of these narratives. If the interviews are analysed according to the categorical-form approach, whereby sections or single words belonging to a defined category are collected from texts emanating from a number of narrative actors (Lieblich et al. 1998: 12–13), then a newsroom narrative emerges (or, to be more precise, a foreign news desk narrative) – an aggregate narrative as opposed to the discrete ones of the individual journalists. In this narrative, five themes, or what Riessman would call underlying propositions, are discernible.

The first has to do with the importance of identification, of incorporating the perspective of ordinary people in news reporting about the outside world and showing viewers individuals to whom they can relate. 'Being around ordinary people is important', said the Latin American/Asian correspondent. It is good if a report 'conveys how people on site experience their reality', said the youngest of the three women interviewed. A journalist can 'use ordinary people that you can identify with', let them be aware that 'this can happen to me too', said the European correspondent. 'People want to see themselves', said the former Moscow correspondent: a report should be about, or interest, 'Lars in Ludvika' – the Swedish equivalent of Joe the Plumber – and his auntie.

The second theme has to do with the tone of voice in which the correspondent should tell his or her stories to the (wo)man on the couch. 'It shouldn't feel like breaking news', said the shoulders-down correspondent. 'You shouldn't speak too loudly.' Swedish journalists 'want to be offstage, like an invisible choir', stated the Moscow correspondent, echoing what several of his colleagues had said less poetically. A good report should engage the viewer and not leave him or her with 'seventeen unanswered questions', but the viewer would seem to be thought capable of making up his or her own mind about the issues presented. 'Who has given me the right to tell people how to think?' is a response that reveals a good deal about the journalist's view of the audience.

The third theme to emerge from all the interviews is the notion that the reporting country is not the centre of the universe, and that members of this particular national culture have a lot to learn from others. 'We in Sweden are still our little edge of the world', said the German correspondent: 'we are not better than they are.' Slovakia 'is just as good a country as ours', said the Moscow correspondent, and according to the European correspondent, 'we are just like everybody else in the whole world'.

The fourth theme is structured around the metaphor of meeting: 'we want to get people to meet on an equal level', said the German correspondent, referring to enlargement coverage. The Moscow correspondent used the same word, saying it was a good strategy to 'let the viewers meet their new neighbours'. And the younger woman stressed the importance of 'reducing the distance between us and them'.

The fifth and final theme to emerge from the discourse of the journalists has to do with the importance of resisting stereotypes. A reporter has to 'highlight positive things, not just problematize', said one of the Swedish journalists. 'You shouldn't confirm people's views. You should continually change the perspective.' Similarly, her younger female colleague emphasized that a journalist should 'widen the viewer's horizons', let the (wo)man on the couch know that 'this is how these people live, this is how they think'.

It is not difficult to relate these newsroom narratives to the notion of cosmopolitanism presented in chapter 1. The question is: can they be related to the narratives in the work they produce, and in particular news narratives of Europe on the eve of EU enlargement? And can they be related to any themes that may emerge from discussions with the people for whom these news stories were intended? These are the questions to be addressed in the next two sections.

News narratives of European enlargement

As can be seen from table 3.1, the *Rapport* broadcasts on which this chapter focuses contained a total of 203 news items, including both telegrams and reports that varied in length from 1 to 7 minutes. Ten

Table 3.1 Distribution of reports about Europe in SVT's *Rapport*, 26 April – 9 May 2004

Distribution of material	No.	%
Total number of news items	203	100
Number of news items about Europe (telegrams plus longer items)	49	24
Number of news items about Europe a minute or more in length	27	13
Number of items pertaining to EU enlargement (including telegrams)	21	10
Total time of news items (in minutes)	371	100
Total time of news items about Europe a minute or more in length (in minutes)	88	24

per cent of the items in this particular sample had to do with EU enlargement, and 24 per cent had to do with events taking place in Europe or involving Europeans. For the narrative analysis, a selection was made of all news items of at least a minute in length that pertained to Europe, European countries or Europeans. Together, these thirteen items represent 25 per cent of all broadcast time.

As argued in earlier chapters, the question of what the world looks like when refracted through one's television screen cannot be answered simply by looking at what goes on there. It is also necessary to ask who populates that world. Apart from the many figures referred to and glimpsed in the background, the twenty-seven items about Europe in this sample contained interviews with a wide range of people, including a waitress, a worker and an entrepreneur from Estonia; a farmer, environmental activists and engineers from Poland; a young, blue-jeaned Lithuanian lawyer; a Latvian optician and an economist working for a Swedish bank in Riga; a middle-aged woman who said: 'In my view we've always been part of Europe. This is our place. It's where we belong', and a young Polish woman who explained to the reporter that enlargement was a good thing because 'our country will be opened up to other cultures and European countries. It's important for young people to be able to study and work wherever they want.' The variety of voices and faces is more easily overviewed when organized in the form of table 3.2.

Table 3.2 The different sorts of people interviewed in SVT's *Rapport* news
items about Europe of a minute or more in length, 26 April – 9 May 2004

Category	No.	% of all actors
Workers, people in service industries, students, pensioners, 'men on the street'	26	33
Entrepreneurs, engineers, management	19	24
Officials and politicians (including government members, foreign heads of state, municipal officials, trade unionists, police, and eight Swedish EU parliamentarians)	32	40.5
Experts	2	2.5
Total	79	100

What table 3.2 does not take into account is which of these
interviewees can be judged to be the 'primary definers' of the news
stories in which they appear and which occupy the most space. If
these things are taken into account, the first two categories in the
table become more prominent. Even if they are not, it is clear that
'ordinary people' and the middle and entrepreneurial class of the
new member states are a notable presence in these reports. This
would seem to provide confirmation of the strategies spoken of in
the newsroom, to give viewers people to whom they can relate.

Two recurrent themes are discernible in the news stories about
Europe contained in *Rapport* during this period. In one, enlargement is framed as a threat; in the other it is framed as a source of
potential. In the first of these themes, three risks associated with
enlargement are outlined: the threat posed to Swedish jobs and
welfare by cheap labour migrants from the new member states;
the influx of crime from 'the East' accompanying the relaxation of
border controls; and the opening of the floodgates for cheap alcohol
(here Swedish 'alco-tourists' were repeatedly depicted as blithely
crossing the Baltic to stock up, delighted at having found such
bargains in liquor stores on the other side of the sea). The theme
originates in the political discourse prevailing in Sweden during
this time. The second theme paints a different picture of enlargement, and it is perhaps not unreasonable to argue that it originated
in the *Rapport* newsroom (and the field in which SVT journalists

work). Four examples of reports exemplifying the enlargement-as-potential theme will be presented in what follows.

Estonian manpower agencies

In one of these reports, viewers were told that Estonian manpower agencies had found an inexpensive way of getting around the transition rules that several EU countries were planning to impose by renting out cheap labour from their home base. The journalist visited one of the agencies that had 'mushroomed' on the eve of enlargement and talked to the Swedish-speaking Estonian who owned the agency, a man who wanted to go abroad to improve his income, and a young waitress who was interested in finding out how other people lived. She wanted to go to Finland because it is 'another country, a different country. I'd like to get new experiences and see how the Finns really are.'

From an optimistic, proactive Estonia, the viewer's gaze was directed back to Sweden, where the prime minister could be seen warning in parliament about 'social tourism', and where a trade unionist expressed concern about what such labour migration would mean.

This is what could be called an 'open text', in that different readers could make different sense of it. A Swedish construction worker could well be thought to pay most attention to what the trade unionist said, and find the prospect of encountering an Estonian at his workplace a matter of concern. A young Swede, however, could be thought to identify with the nineteen-year-old waitress, who was prepared to venture abroad in search of new experiences, and who was not depicted as threatening. It is worth noting that she was a key figure in this story, while an implied Swedish construction worker (or waitress) was absent. As an open text, the evaluation is also open: the Estonians are not presented in a threatening light, but the summing up would seem to say that this was no straightforward issue. In any case, an impression with which the viewer may have been left was that these new members were outgoing and enterprising, while Swedes were conservative and unprepared for change.

The ecological Polish farmer

In another item, viewers were told that the modernization of agriculture was turning out to be a fateful issue for the entire Baltic region. Polish farms were small and environmentally friendly, but changes were required if they were going to be able to compete with agriculture in the rest of Europe. The 'abstract' of the narrative that followed was basically that, when it came to farming, Poland was preparing to enter the EU as an old-fashioned but respectable member. The 'complicating action' consisted in the fateful question: Would its modernization turn it into an environmental abuser, like farmers in Sweden and elsewhere in the EU, as it caught up with the others with the help of artificial fertilizers?

Aided by reporter voiceovers, the story was told by a farmer, Barbara, who was interviewed in a field on her farm outside Gliwice. She was worried that small farmers would disappear with EU membership, and hoped that Poles would avoid the mistakes of the European Union when it came to overproduction. Another woman, an environmental activist, said there were hopes that organic farming in Poland would develop further, and that the challenge facing Polish farmers was to aid this development. According to this woman and the reporter, should Poland industrialize its farming, the fate of the Baltic lay in the balance. It was Barbara, the farmer, who gave the evaluation: 'The future is not bright for us all, but those who are prepared to work and put their heart in it will succeed.'

There seems to be a subtext in this report, as if the journalist was saying to the viewer: 'This isn't what you expected, is it?' In the first place, in this text Poland was a model country, rather than a wannabe with a lot to learn from a purportedly environmentally friendly country like Sweden. The hope expressed by all who had a voice in this story was that Poland would not become a polluter like its counterpart on the other side of the Baltic. In the second place, the actors and primary definers in this story were both women, which could challenge the stereotype of Poland as a male-dominated society. Neither was presented as an anomaly. The story, in other words, would seem to offer new perspectives, challenge stereotypes, and resist confirming people's views – to use the words of one of the SVT journalists encountered in the preceding section.

The Polish engineer

Men did, of course, feature in news stories about the new member states in general, and in Poland in particular. In another item addressing the problem of the environment, four men were interviewed: two engineers, a member of the Polish Green Party, and the head of the municipal water company in the city of Krakow. In the 'abstract' of this story, viewers were told that the environment was the area that was going to require the heaviest investment when the EU's new members come to harmonize with the rest of the Union. Poland, the biggest of the new member states, also had the biggest environmental problems, but was investing heavily in sewage treatment plants. The 'complicating action' was introduced when the Green Party member challenged the view of the municipal official that as much was being done as possible. It was an exchange familiar from the Swedish political context.

What is interesting about this particular story is its subplot. The primary definer – the man whose account opened the story and who provided the evaluation that ended it – was an engineer who had recently returned to Poland after twenty years as an émigré. To him, the sewage treatment plant he was building, and which would clean up the accumulated poison of generations, was a symbol of the 'new' Poland. 'When I came back', he explained, 'it was a different country. For us it was like a second emigration because it felt like we'd come to a different country, with different mentality, different needs, with development we couldn't imagine, and now we're adding more to this.' In the past, he said, people looked and saw only industrial development, and they were proud of it, because of the propaganda. But now when they looked around them they saw problems and wanted to make improvements. They were sorting their waste, and this, he said, was promising.

The symbolism is unmistakeable: apart from the metaphor of 'cleaning up the waste' of generations, there is the interesting image of the émigré encountering a new country when he returns home.

Given that Sweden, since the end of the nineteenth century, has been a nation of emigrants (some of whom remained in their new domiciles, others of whom returned), it was interesting to find out whether this theme found any resonance 'on the couch'.

The Lithuanian entrepreneur

In the final example to be sketched here, the success story of Lithuania – the 'tiger' of Europe, viewers were told, and one of the fastest growing economies in the world – was related from the vantage point of Tomas Juska, an entrepreneur who was twenty-one years old when the country became independent. With four classmates and no money, he started a flooring company that now had an annual turnover of half a billion kronor. Juska described Lithuania using the following points of reference: 'We are a society of 3.5 million people and on our roads there are about 1.2 million cars. I can pay for parking by sending an SMS message and our mobile phone penetration is more than 60 per cent. Just these few examples tell how healthy our economy is.' Unease that Sweden would be invaded by Lithuanians who wanted to piggyback on the welfare system feels distant here, said the reporter in a voiceover, before introducing the disequilibrium. One million people still lived in poverty (this to a shot of a man with his horse and plough in the fields); it took Juska twelve years to scrape together the money for his dream house (up to which he could be seen driving in a new car); and it would take another fifteen years for the whole country to attain the average EU living standard. In the elegant living rooms of his house, with brandy and a cordless phone on the table beside him, Juska spoke less of what Lithuania hoped to get from the EU ('it is a nice label', he said) than what his country could offer the Union: 'I believe we can give to all the Europe, more developed Europe, our hunger, our energy, our readiness to work hard, and I would say exploit these things. Because otherwise not only we will maintain as province, all Europe will maintain as province in global processes [*sic*]. So the only way is to put together our strengths.'

Even more clearly than in the other three stories, personification strategies are put to use in this item. The Lithuanian tiger is embodied in the self-confident, energetic businessman, who although young is already established. What is interesting here is that, despite the disequilibrium of continued poverty for a third of the population, the dominant theme of the report is 'ask not what Europe can do for Lithuania, ask what Lithuania can do for Europe', to paraphrase John F. Kennedy (just as the inaugural words of Barack Obama would echo those of the Polish engineer, who saw his country dusting itself off and remaking itself). Unlike the open text in which the Estonian waitress figured, this can be seen as a 'closed text' – i.e. one which urges the viewer to see the situation in one rather than several ways. This brings to mind the comment by one of the SVT journalists about giving their viewers a 'red thread' to hold onto.

Narratives of European enlargement: summary

These four texts – and others in the sample – draw on the naturalist tradition in telling the story of various 'new Europeans'. It is the accounts of the Estonian waitress, the Polish farmer, the returning émigré and the Lithuanian entrepreneur which further the narratives in which they are actors. The perspective throughout is that of new member states (and, more precisely, inhabitants of new member states) looking into the European family they are about to join, rather than of established union members on the inside looking out.

An unmistakable feature of these stories is the determination and energy with which the encounter with other Europeans is contemplated by these new neighbours. The Swedes in these news items, by way of contrast, tend to be sceptical and on their guard (in the case of some leading politicians, trade unionists, customs officials and police officers) or irresponsible (in the case of the alco-tourists). It is not inconceivable that, compared with the dynamic newcomers, they would come across to culturally competent viewers as conservative.

Nevertheless, there are repeated occasions on which the Swedish viewer is invited to identify with his or her counterparts on the other side of the Baltic, who, for example, are beginning to buy ecological food and sort their waste, who are filmed eating at elegant restaurants and walking city streets in designer jeans rather than tramping along on foot behind a horse and plough, as was the case in the mid-1990s. Nor are these entirely foreign countries, the viewer is invited to note, through shots of a familiar grocery store chain and Swedish banks in Latvia.

The question, however, is whether evidence of such identification can be found. How does the average viewer make sense of such news stories, if in fact he or she takes notice of them at all? Focus group interviews in the weeks that followed the broadcasting of these and the other *Rapport* news stories in the sample presented in chapter 2 sought an answer to that question.

The view from the couch

The focus group study was intended to generate insights both into how people make sense of the outside world and into how the media might contribute to that sense-making – i.e. the role that television reports could be thought to play in developing mental 'maps'. It included groups of pensioners, workers, musicians and librarians in the small Swedish town and corresponding groups in the capital, 300 kilometres to the north, plus a group of farmers (an equivalent of which was not found in Stockholm). While concerned to exclude obvious candidates for cosmopolitanism such as political elites, university academics, activists and businessmen, no attempt was made to include, exclude, or even find out whether groups contained, people who were particularly bound to local environments or who had experience of living and working abroad. It can thus be seen as a finding, rather than a methodological problem, that this approach fished up many people with what could be thought of as cosmopolitan experiences. Walking into the pensioners' collective in a Stockholm suburb or a local branch of the library, I found myself talking to people who had lived in Africa; in the countryside I found myself talking to a farmer who helped a Swiss friend deliver dairy equipment to Chinese entrepreneurs; in the little town, music teachers and dairy workers told me about how they travelled to Germany every summer to play in the symphonic band and discuss war experiences with their elderly hosts. In every group, people with origins outside the country made their presence felt, in several cases by their participation – be they a Finnish librarian or an American or Polish musician. It ultimately occurred to me that to put together a 'pure' sample of Swedes without experience of the world beyond the borders of their nation would have been to construct a problem of representativity, not the other way around. In sum, the 'go fishing' method was found fruitful and defensible. While more, and perhaps larger, groups would have been an advantage, it should be pointed out that there is no definite answer to how many people should be interviewed in a good focus group study (Stokes 2003: 151).

An attempt was made in these discussions to leave open the question of how the outside world (*omvärld*, as opposed to *värld* or 'world') was to be defined, as it was the respondents' definitions that were of interest. The conversation started with the question of what came to mind when the word 'home' was mentioned, and progressed to what they associated with the words 'community', 'EU' and 'outside world', with follow-up questions in between these key points in the discussion. Other questions probed where respondents got images of these things from, if they travelled, where and why, and if they ever felt at home when somewhere else. Finally, their media consumption habits were discussed, and whether they ever felt that they recognized, or felt connected to, the people in news reports about other countries.

The farmers readily gave an account of themselves as men who have stayed close to home throughout their lives. When it came to the EU, a farmer who had actually travelled extensively in Europe in an earlier occupation said: 'I think I feel a bit far away. You are too far away from it somehow. So it's hard to take it to your heart.'

Interlocutor: Enlargement, or the EU in general? It feels . . .?
Farmer 1: The EU feels far away. Enlargement too, I think.
Farmer 2: The EU feels so bureaucratic, I think. [*The others murmur agreement.*] It's just a lot of bureaucrats who sit in Brussels and decide everything.

Farmer 3: This is the way I see it. The bigger we get, the closer to downfall we come. If you look at it historically, *no* one big constellation has held. You can go back to the Mayas, Incas, Roman Empire, Soviet Union, whatever you like: *everything falls apart* in the end. Because you can never unite so many different cultures and so many different ways of doing things under one and the same roof.

Interlocutor: So it's not just the practical aspects of enlargement but also the cultural . . .

Farmer 3: Yes, it is, it's like, if you look at our own sector, if we were to have a common seed date in the entire EU, should the Greeks sow the same day as they do in northern Sweden? [*Slams his coffee cup onto the saucer for emphasis.*] There's a bunch of people down there in Brussels calling all the shots, and they're . . . they're not living in the real world.

Interlocutor: Your image of the EU, is it bureaucrats then?

Farmer 1: Yes, exactly. That's the picture. When it comes to enlargement, I think there's going to be . . . how to put it, there will be a bigger difference between them . . . how should I put it?

Farmer 3: I know what you mean.

Farmer 1: The East, the Baltics, are a bit farther down, and then we have the others who are a bit higher up. This, there'll be too big a difference, there'll be too big a range now. The gap between the good and the less good will be even bigger.

Interlocutor: An A- and B-team?

Farmer 1: Yeah, maybe you could call it that. Then the B-team wants to grow up to the A-team's level, but then the A-team has to pay for it somehow.

As can be seen from this excerpt, a clear 'other' emerges in the discussion with the farmers: the bureaucrats in Brussels. The latter are not alone, however, but have the Swedish government for company, as well as the rich landowners who are seen as running the Swedish Farmers' Union, all of whom are pitted against an 'us' that is comprised of the 'little people'. The key actors in the stories of the farmers are the government, the bureaucrats in Brussels, and taxes and subsidies. The discourse is materialist, rather than one characterized by ideas or visions. As to the human actors on the other side of the Baltic Sea, they are absences rather than presences in this talk. Shown the report about the Polish farmer presented in the preceding section, they did not comment on her situation at all, in terms either of recognizing it or failing to recognize it, but they *did* relate the item to their own problems and situation. The question is: Is this evidence that the news item does not touch them, or is it evidence of the invisibility of the conventions at work in it, rendering them oblivious to the personification/identification strategies but immediately 'internalizing' the text by associating it with their own situation?

Hostility towards the EU and Brussels bureaucrats does not necessarily find a twin in hostility to the outside world and non-Swedes in general, it is interesting to note:

> *Farmer:* Everyone who talks about the EU, about how it's all about justice and peace, they seem to forget that the EU is building a wall around itself.
> *Interlocutor:* And what do you think of that?
> *Farmer:* I think it is utter nonsense. There we are, you know, either we're going to open outwards. Or else I don't understand what they want.

But this particular farmer *did* find one good thing about the EU and, by corollary, enlargement:

> What I think is positive about the EU is this possibility to travel, you know, in an easier way. Because travel, I've always been fascinated by that, and I like different people, different food cultures, where there are all sorts of things. It is fascinating. It's enriching, quite simply.

This exchange suggests that a cosmopolitan outlook can thrive even when rooted physically and discursively in a particular patch of a particular countryside, by people who are clearly sceptical about one of the major projects of political cosmopolitanism in this era: the European Union.

The farmers told stories of going away and coming back – one grandparent, for example, had tried living the life of the émigré in the US once upon a time, before giving up and heading back to his Swedish homestead – and the farmers themselves had travelled abroad and felt it right to be back home. This theme is also in evidence in the discussion with the musicians who left their small town to study in the capital and went on to work with major orchestras in big cities abroad, but who had made conscious decisions to give it all up for the quiet, good life of teaching music at the local school. Like the farmers, the musicians in the small town readily depicted themselves as provincials, rooted in their community, and it was only in passing, and in response to gently reiterated questions, that it emerged that they had in fact been abroad, living, for example, with older Germans while on a symphonic band exchange, and quizzing their hosts about how the Second World War looked and felt from the other side. In one way, such activity is not unrelated to the work of the cosmopolitan, who is open to vantage points that are not his or her own. In another way, these experiences seem to have been anything other than essential to these particular respondents, even in a discussion devoted to their views of the outside world.

The point to be made here is not that indications of cosmopolitanism are lacking in this discussion. Rather, it is that they contain evidence of non-cosmopolitanism (not to be confused with anti-cosmopolitanism, which can be thought to have more to do with fundamentalism and xenophobia). These men are quite simply satisfied with their situation and can see no reason to improve it or to share it with others. This is evident in talk of the EU, for example.

Interlocutor: If I say the word 'EU', what sort of pictures do you get in your head?
Small-town Musician 1: [chuckles] Red tape. It's mostly negative actually.
Small-town Musician 2: Yep. The first time, when we were going to vote on the EU, then it was mostly focused on how great . . .
Small-town Musician 1: [*interrupting*] I don't understand why they tried that one on, when we have it so good here anyway. We managed on our own, like, we had . . . I don't get it, we had no need of Europe.
Interlocutor: Does it still feel the same?
Small-town Musician 1: Of course it does. It feels more like we're being used by others, if you know what I mean. Because it costs a lot to be in now.

Small-town Musician 2: Right. Plus there's such a state apparatus down there, with thousands of employees . . .

Small-town Musician 1: . . . social, secure networks, networks that we have here in society anyway: what's going to happen with them now, when there's going to be more and more coming who *don't* have that, if you know what I mean? Will we be *worse* off, like? There's unease. You feel uneasy about it. So there's nothing positive in it.

Interlocutor: Nothing at all?

Small-town Musician 1: No.

Interlocutor: If you think about . . . the French or British and so on, you don't think us, that's us?

Small-town Musician 1: I don't know.

Small-town Musician 2: Sure. We're Europeans. So you have a certain community.

The first of these two musicians, in particular, gives expression to attitudes that could be described as the opposite of cosmopolitan, if cosmopolitanism is given the dictionary definition of 'excessive imitation of traits of others at the expense of the integrity of one's own land', or someone who learns to live with diversity in modes of thought and ways of life. His views are more in keeping with the opposite: 'provincial, local, limited or restricted by the attitudes, interests or loyalties of a single region'.

A rather different pattern emerged in the discussion with four librarians, who, as they themselves joked, represented all the generations of working life, as two were in late middle age, with grown children, one was heavily pregnant, and one, barely out of her teens, was just finishing her studies. Compared with the participants in the other four focus groups in the small town, who tended to give static replies, these women were quick to build on the responses of their colleagues, interweave story with story, and note the connections they themselves had made to earlier contributions to the discussion. Emotions could run high, as, for example, when speaking of the frustration they experienced as news consumers:

Librarian 1: The awful thing about TV news is that you stop thinking. I mean, I've almost *stopped* looking at the news because of that. I think there is *report* after *report* after *report*, and I don't have a chance to react. That it's like that. So I much prefer to watch, you know, *slower* programmes and reportage . . . when you keep up, like. Because it's . . . it's pure violence. I mean it's terror, terror, terror. And maimed people.

Interlocutor: And you mean that it's not enough just to know what's going on, it's important to react somehow?

Librarian 1: Yes, for *me* it's important to react. Because I think sitting and being spoon-fed and not reacting, it's somehow . . . well, you feel numbed. And anything at all can happen without you reacting in the end.

Interlocutor: And the image you get of the outside world from TV news is a lot of conflict and war then?

Librarian 1: *Absolutely.*

The problematic relationship these women experienced with the media, or with what has been referred to as 'images from elsewhere', is vividly illustrated in responses to questions of whether they had ever felt 'at home' when abroad. The experiences that sprang immediately to their minds were the very opposite, yet clearly relevant to the dynamics of sense-making being explored here. One occasion was the murder, in September 2003, of the former Swedish foreign minister Anna Lindh; the other was the murder one bright spring morning by escaped convicts of two policemen in the idyllic nearby town of Malexander. The librarians told the following stories about what happened when they received the news:

Librarian 1: I was in England, you see, and it was *awful*. We were a group of librarians in England, who suddenly got the news. And we stood there and felt completely *outside*. We wanted to be *home* when it happened. And we *cried* together and it was . . . it was *awfully* strange. And then you saw all those pictures on TV, crying people, and you felt that *that's* where we should be. It was . . . it was strange. I got behind.

Librarian 2: I know, it was the same with the police murders.

Librarian 1: Exactly.

Librarian 2: And it took a long time before I caught up. On the airplane there were *Dagens Nyheter* and *Svenska Dagbladet* [*leading Swedish*

newspapers], and it was all about my little home town Malexander.
It was so strange, it was so far away to read all about that. And then
everybody had to talk about it and I wanted to hear where everyone
had been and what everyone had experienced, to be able to keep up
somehow.
Librarian 3: It was strange.
Librarian 2: [*to one of her colleagues*] But what you said about news, it's
. . . it's so strange when you see lots of people, because obviously, all
that about 9/11, it's stuff you just stand and think about for a long,
long, long time, about individual cases and so on. But otherwise it's
war and so on, when you see that there are lots of people dying, and
you aren't moved as much as when you see *one* single story, *one* person
who tells it. It's like you say, you have to distance yourself, you have
to screen yourself off . . .
Librarian 3: It feels so hopeless. I think you have to . . . I think you
have to try to distance yourself and come back to your own little
reality and try, well, do the best you can with your own little life.
That's where we usually end up when we discuss things. Sometimes
we discuss all the misery, but we try to do what we can in our own
little library.

There are many insights to be gleaned from this dialogue, not
least when it comes to the work of imagination. For these women,
it is not enough to follow the aftermath of the murders in the
media, or from afar. Despite all that is said about the 'breaking
news' pace of reporting, these women felt they would not be able
to 'catch up' until they were back home. They reflected on their
relationship to media reporting, found it problematic, and claimed
they ultimately removed their gaze from the turbulent world
outside, to which they apparently felt some sort of responsibility,
and returned to their 'little library'.

Another difference between these women and the men in the
other focus groups in the small town is their tendency to talk about
people, rather than rules and regulations. When asked what they
think of when the word 'EU' is mentioned, they immediately
bring up enlargement, which in this case was understood as a
broadening of their own horizons – a 'going out' of Swedes rather
than a coming in of new members.

Librarian 2: I think . . . I think it feels positive. It's like [Librarian 1] says with the new countries, above all the younger generation, that they want to get out and travel more and get in touch. And it's also the case that Sweden is too small a country for many who have lived here their entire lives. They think the whole world looks like this. And that we do the right thing and that it's best here, and all that. I think we can learn a lot from each other and . . . I think it's good that . . . we broaden somehow . . . that people . . . that we can travel easily between countries and see how others do things and pick up the good things and the bad things, or good things. Yeah, I think it's good. I think it feels positive. And I also think, when you look at the celebrations, you know, from those countries that haven't had it so easy, you can feel, bah, it's so *good* that they are joining now, they are really wonderful and celebrate and all that. Somehow they must have felt like second-class people all the time. We've had so much, we've had it so good and all that, and everything for them has been a bit worse. It feels . . . *I'd* feel like that if I lived in that country and saw how everyone else had it.

Librarian 1: I think they're going to go really, really far now: it's going to be the rest of us left standing there and . . . cheering. [*All laugh.*] Or trying to keep up with them. Because I can almost *feel* how they want revenge, now they can try too and . . . be as good as the others [. . .] You can imagine these people who have so much, a lot of knowledge and potential to be something – they haven't been able to, because they live in a country where there aren't those possibilities. And suddenly the possibilities are there. Yes, I can really see before my eyes how they are going to work to be . . . better.

Librarian 2: It's going to be exciting to see. You *really* admire them. I saw a programme about a computer guy, with a computer company in Poland I think it was, a *big* company, with *lots* of people. It was so . . . fantastic.

Interlocutor: What programme was that?

Librarian 2: It was on . . . some news programme.

There is an interesting contrast between this exchange and the first one between the librarians excerpted above. While the first exchange would seem to indicate the presence of a certain degree of resistance to media messages and the various strategies of journalists, the image of the new EU members that emerges from the passage above is very much in keeping with that which emanates from the textual analysis of the Swedish television news items presented earlier, and the interviews with the Swedish journalists themselves. So while, on the one hand, the librarian feels she has become immune to news reports of a violent world, she would appear, on the other, to be making sense of other news – such as the meaning of enlargement – in a way that accords with the journalistic narratives (both verbal and textual). There is evidence, in the talk of these women, of identification with individuals in news reports from abroad rather than with the many thousands who are in trouble (to paraphrase the second librarian). For want of a better label, this could be called the woman with the Samsonite suitcase syndrome, and it is worth considering whether it is as problematic as the librarians think it is. It could be evidence of cosmopolitan susceptibilities or a symptom of the difficulties that may be encountered on the way to forming a cosmopolitan outlook.

Relating the stories

A feature of these and the other focus group discussions that has not been documented here is that, in the discourse of the respondents, globalization emerges as something natural, almost organic, while the EU is artificial, the product of a bureaucratic inclination to complicate the life of the average person, and an entity held together by red tape. Another feature is that 'home' is somewhere secure and pleasant. Its opposite, 'not-home', is not a place full of foreigners, but a place defined by the presence of conflict and violence.

The discussions excerpted here suggest that we should not be hasty about concluding that mediated worldliness is the most important factor when it comes to making sense of the world and relations with people beyond the borders of the nation. In these and other discussions, face-to-face interactions with Chinese entrepreneurs and Asian tobacconists in London, and talking to people who were 'at home' when Lindh was killed or in Germany when

Hitler was waging war, leave their impression on the respondents and come more easily to mind than flashbacks from news reports when discussing their 'take' on the world. How these face-to-face and mediated interactions work together, or conflict with one another, is something worthy of more scholarly consideration. But there is evidence here of the connections Giddens (1991: 7) writes about between individual experience and abstract systems, such as the EU.

Judging from this small excursion into a realm populated by the target audience of one of the broadcasters featured in this book, cosmopolitans can be found behind the desk at the local library, among other places (such as the pensioners' collective and among the Stockholm musicians). They can also be found in the Swedish Television newsroom, at least in that corner of it occupied by the foreign news desk. This is hardly a surprise – as Hannerz (2004b: 2) has noted, foreign correspondents are 'key players in today's globalization of consciousness'. And, indeed, any other result would have been disquieting. What is striking here is, rather, the clear stance adopted in their reporting in the week before the fireworks and Beethoven of 1 May. Enlargement was a Good Thing in the view of these journalists, and their message was that Swedes and the inhabitants of other member states should be prepared to welcome these new family members and recognize them as kin. This emerged not only from interviews with the journalists but also from analysis of the reports they produced during this period.

The question is whether the journalists and librarians share cosmopolitan perspectives because both these groups have similar political and moral outlooks, or because the librarians have been looking at the world through the window of SVT news reports for the greater part of their lives: in other words, is this evidence of situated culture or mediated culture at work? Whatever the answer to that question may be (and it is, of course, a question that cannot be satisfactorily answered), both these groups would seem to be engaged in the social practice Appadurai had in mind, a practice that may be called the work of cosmopolitan imagination.

4

A Wave of Cosmopolitan Sentiment: Television Coverage of the Asian Tsunami

'Throw your arms around the world', the singers in the celebrity charity Band Aid urged people in December 2004, as they had during so many Christmastides in the past. They sang about a world outside the windows of their listeners that was full of fear rather than plenty – a world in which tears were the only water flowing. On Boxing Day those familiar words took on new meaning. But the reference to a lack of water struck a discordant note, as it was quite the opposite which brought 'dread and fear' to twelve countries in Southeast Asia and countless people whose homes were elsewhere but who, or whose friends and loved ones, had been holidaying in the region when the tsunami struck, claiming 230,000 lives, injuring more, and leaving untold numbers homeless and deprived of their livelihood.

Triggered by an earthquake in the Indian Ocean off the western coast of northern Sumatra, the giant wave devastated the shores of Indonesia, Sri Lanka, southern India and Thailand and caused deaths as far away as Port Elizabeth in South Africa. Indonesia had the highest death toll, losing almost 127,000 of its inhabitants, followed by Sri Lanka (38,000), India (16,000),

Thailand (11,000), Somalia, Burma, the Maldives, Malaysia, Tanzania, the Seychelles, Bangladesh, South Africa, Yemen and Kenya. A week after the flood wave hit, some 5,000 European holidaymakers were still missing, including about 1,000 Swedes and as many Germans, 700 Italians, 440 Britons, 462 Norwegians, 419 Danes and 263 Finns (in each case the number of dead was later revised downwards).

The tsunami caught the attention of people everywhere for a moment – a rather long moment in the world's otherwise short attention span – and resulted in an unprecedented outpouring of solidarity. Aid pledges from governments and private donations from individuals across the planet surpassed any effort seen since the end of the Second World War. People were paying, as well as praying, for 'the other ones', to paraphrase the Band Aid song. Asked, a fortnight after the tidal wave hit, what was so remarkable about the crisis it had left in its wake, UN Secretary General Kofi Annan replied that, above all, 'it happened in real time, and it was on television, and on the front of newspapers. [. . .] Everybody saw the human tragedy.'[1]

Annan calls attention here to an important feature of the crisis that makes it of interest to scholars of both globalization and the media: that simultaneity of experience associated with the notion of 'time–space compression' (Harvey 1990). But it also bears a striking affinity with Beck's observation that certain events are played out in the sphere of 'global domestic politics, with the whole of humanity participating simultaneously through the mass media' (2006: 2). As noted in chapter 1, Beck thinks that people can become cosmopolitans by default, as a side-effect of circumstances over which they have no control. The question that interests him – but to which he arguably fails to give a satisfactory answer – is when and, above all, how such 'unconscious' or latent cosmopolitanism becomes conscious or active and gives rise to a global public (ibid.: 34).

News reporting of the tsunami offers a particularly compelling opportunity to study this. While chapter 2 compared the way national broadcasters, on the one hand, and global broadcasters, on the other, tell viewers about their world on a day-to-day basis, this chapter takes a look at how such workers of the imagination behaved during what could be called a 'cosmopolitan moment'.

From a somewhat different point of entry, it continues to question the assumption that global broadcasters are those most liable to foster cosmopolitan sentiments, and asks whether journalists addressing national audiences in their safe, dry front rooms might be as, if not more, capable of using a cosmopolitan vocabulary to speak to their viewers. There are more comparisons involved here, however, than that between global and national broadcasters. The differences in coverage of the tsunami by journalists from different cultures is also of interest, because nations mourn in different ways, just as individuals do.

The notions of media ritual and mediatization come into play at this point. Where scholars of disaster reporting such as Quarantelli (1989), Elliot (1989) and Wilkins (1989, 1985) have focused on the media in their role as information relayers, television is seen here as having a less tangible but more compelling sort of power, as explained earlier. This is performative, and has to do with the medium's capacity to stimulate cohesion.

After conferring with Beck and Boltanski – one of the first to relate media portrayals of distant suffering to cosmopolitanism – results of an analysis of the more than 900 reports filed by eight broadcasters on the tsunami will be presented to see how different sense could be made of the human tragedy that, according to Kofi Annan, 'everybody' saw. It will be argued that, while a meta-narrative emerged of a world mourning together and collectively doing its bit to alleviate suffering, there were interesting differences in reporting when it came to messages about who the players were in the new cosmopolitan world that emerged, if only for a moment, in the wake of the giant wave.

Passive cosmopolitanization and its activation

Beck, as will be recalled, argues that cosmopolitanism has ceased to be solely philosophical and is now reality, with the human condition itself having become cosmopolitan. He distinguishes, however, between two varieties. One is more akin to the philosophical phenomenon, is active and associated with ideals and certain views of humanity and political organization. Beck refers to this as cosmopolitanism or the 'cosmopolitan outlook'. The other variety is unconscious or passive, and is referred to by Beck as the product of 'really existing cosmopolitanization' (2006: 19).

The cosmopolitan in the latter sense of the word is someone who has ended up in this condition for reasons not of his or her own choosing, or as a result of 'uncontrollable events that merely befall us' (Beck 2006: 20). It *may* involve choice, however, as cosmopolitanization is a side-effect not only of risk and interdependence but also of consumerism. Cultural difference sells well, Beck writes. Elements from many different countries are continually compared and combined; ordinary people effortlessly switch cultures and 'experiential domains'; they develop 'everyday practices and skills to deal with a high degree of interdependence and globality' (ibid.: 41–2). It is not difficult to apply these indicators to the Europeans who consume media products from all over the world, eat sushi, and regularly look forward to spending a couple of winter weeks in Thailand. The intriguing question is: What happens when such experiences become linked with the vicarious?

Acknowledging the inevitability of cosmopolitanization does not mean that everyone is a good cosmopolitan, in Beck's view. The 'really existing' variety is in fact a deformed one, and the undercurrent of his writing is a normative yearning for its mobilization, for a transformation to a more widespread cosmopolitan outlook. In Beck's account, this outlook is characterized by a 'historically alert, reflexive awareness' and by a 'global sense, a sense of boundarylessness' (2006: 2). There is nothing new, he reminds us, about the mixing of cultures. What is new is an awareness of it, 'its self-conscious political affirmation, its reflection and recognition before a global public via the mass media, in the news' and in global social movements (ibid.: 21). In a world in which cosmopolitan norms prevail, 'a shared space of responsibility and agency' that bridges national borders is created. Here, political action among strangers takes place in ways that are familiar from national political settings.

Two of what Beck identifies as the constitutive principles of the cosmopolitan outlook are of particular interest here. One has to do with how global risks and crises promote an awareness of interdependence and result in a 'civilizational community of fate'. In a world of global crises, 'the old differentiations between internal and external, national and international, us and them, lose their validity and a new cosmopolitan realism becomes essential' (Beck 2006: 14). The other principle is that of 'perspective-taking' – the interchangeability of situations, and 'cosmopolitan empathy' (ibid.: 7). This has to do with the capacity and willingness to put oneself in the position of the victim, something Beck attributes in large part to the media. 'The spaces of our emotional imagination have expanded in a transnational sense', he writes; 'suffering is presented in compelling images in the mass media [and] this produces cosmopolitan pity which forces us to act' (ibid.: 6).

Or does it? The causal chain is perhaps not as direct as Beck would have it. While he could no doubt find countless examples to illustrate his thesis, a sceptic such as Moeller (1999) could find as many or more to counter it – wars, humanitarian crises and natural disasters that have aroused little or no response from the viewer inhabiting a transnational emotional space. Chouliaraki, as mentioned earlier, has identified a 'pessimistic narrative' which blames the technology of television for distancing audiences from their counterparts in faraway places, rather than bringing them closer. Editing techniques and repetition keep viewers at arm's length from the event unfolding and the people affected by it; a multitude of channels and the remote control give the person on the couch the possibility of governing his or her own experience.

But Chouliaraki acknowledges the arguments of the 'optimists' too. According to this narrative, television has 'the capacity to establish an imaginary "we" that brings all spectators together in the act of watching'. The very act of viewing brings a common feeling into being, and a sense of responsibility arises on the part of the spectator confronted with images of sufferers who need help from their fellow human beings (2006: 24–9). Although Chouliaraki devotes considerable energy to explicating the problems with this account, her position is that television can provide a space for a cosmopolitan public – a space in which it is possible to act, and not just as a voyeur (ibid.: 199–218).

Cosmopolitanization and media ritual

Pantti (2005) also writes about space and 'democratic feeling communities' that transcend national borders. Noting that an increasing amount of space seems to be devoted to the portrayal of emotion when reporting catastrophes and other tragedies, she writes of how the media have been accused, within the context of a wider debate on 'tabloidization', of spreading 'mourning sickness'. The epithet connotes both a temporary condition and one to which women are prone. Key ingredients are personification, with media consumers invited to identify with one or a few individuals among the masses of humanity's unfortunates, and cultural proximity.

To dismiss such reporting strategies as tabloidization is an easy way out and overlooks an important aspect of media power. Pantti is not the only one to have noted how, at times of public trauma, secondary audiences join the community 'by taking part in the emotions of those who are more directly part of the event' (Pantti 2005: 375). This has often been the case in the era of globalization: she writes about the death of Princess Diana and the murders of the Swedish prime minister Olof Palme and foreign minister Anna Lindh, but 9/11 and the Madrid and London bombings are other familiar examples. Like them, the tsunami – if not the event itself, then the collective grieving that it occasioned – became the sort of media event that Dayan and Katz maintain is capable of achieving social integration 'of the highest order' (1992: 15).

It has already been argued that, to appreciate the power of media actors at such times, it is necessary to attend to their performative role. Cottle (2006) uses the term 'mediatization' to signal how media do not just transmit information about crises but work in more complex ways to enact them. This has a reflexive dimension. Although they do not offer a true substitute for participation in an event or the experience of suffering, as Chouliaraki's pessimists are quick to point out, media actors do give those who were not present the possibility of reflecting on its significance and the prospect of virtual presence. Not least through events like the tsunami, 'media broaden the base of reflexivity through time and space' (Becker 1995: 642). Reflexivity is activated when, for example, television cameras constitute what Becker calls 'peak moments' that 'gather and condense the meanings that are dispersed throughout the rest of the event' (ibid.: 638). As will be seen, this happened a week after the tsunami, when cameras captured Europeans observing three minutes of silence for the victims of the catastrophe, at the same time as the workers of the imagination behind and in front of those cameras invited viewers to participate in the moment of reflection.

Television straddles the spheres of culture, society and politics. Media rituals as well as reporting traditions in general are thought to depend on media actors working 'in concert' with political and social institutions (Elliot 1982; Ettema 2005). This is something to which Durham (2008) has paid attention. Writing of television ritual in the context of American catastrophes, he introduces a useful comparative dimension and contrasts media behaviour at the time of 9/11 with that of Hurricane Katrina, which took the lives of 1,500 people in 2005. The former crisis, he argues, was played out as a traditional media ritual, with television reporting fostering unity between people, media and government. Katrina was different from the traditional media ritual because the media–government consensus was undermined. Government sources were not available to provide the frames to 'resonate' with the meta-narrative of that particular catastrophe (Durham 2008: 99). This raises an interesting issue. How does resonance work at the global level? In a media event such as the tsunami, which *are* the political and social institutions referred to in ritual theory? It is conceivable that they are national (governments that respond to the plight of their own citizens and distant others), global (the UN or world community mobilizing aid), or those of civil society (NGOs responding with relief workers and resources). And what about the individual citizen/viewer? Lewis et al. (2005) argue that this figure has been habitually relegated to the sidelines and written out of the script. As will be seen, there are grounds for suggesting that things may have been different in the case of tsunami reporting. This matter, and its implications for cosmopolitanism, will be returned to later.

To sum up thus far, however: in the attempt to understand the relationship between television and cosmopolitanism through various points of entry, it is useful to consider not just the informational value of news reports but also their performative and ritual roles. A key concept here, once again, is imagination and a key research question is how television may nourish the spectator's imagination of distant suffering.

Nourishing the spectator's imagination

Boltanski asks how, when confronted with suffering thousands of miles away, a person 'comfortably installed in front of the television set in the shelter of the family living room' can form a commitment to action (1999: xv). He is concerned with a 'crisis in pity' which has to do with a loss of confidence in action, 'by a focus on the media and the "spectacle" effects they produce [and] by a temptation to fall back on the community' (ibid.: xvi).

The media, however, need not be a source of apathy or a reason for cynicism. Building on Adam Smith, Boltanski distinguishes between sympathy, which is cut off from suffering by distance in the same way in which a spectator is cut off from the stage in a theatre, and empathy, which is committed rather than detached. The difference between them is accomplished by a reduction in distance by means of the imagination (Boltanksi 1999: 38). This imagination must be nourished, and, writes Boltanski (ibid.: 50), in a line of argumentation parallel to Beck's idea of spaces of emotional imagination, for it to serve the coordination of emotional commitments, different people must be able to nourish their imagination from the same source.

Essential here is the ability to imagine what is impossible, for, without this, pity cannot be formed and shared in the face of someone else's suffering. This ability is related to various forms of expression, of which television reports are one. In such forms 'we find descriptions of the internal states of other people to which we can have no direct access and which by that fact *nourish the imagination* of spectators when faced with distant suffering' (Boltanski 1999: 51). These forms of expression must include descriptions that are 'supple' enough for them to be capable of being applied to other concrete situations 'whose imaginative fleshing out they will promote' (ibid.).

So Boltanski's arguments are that, for the spectator's emotions to be prevented from drifting to the fictional, it is essential that a disposition towards action is maintained, and that action appears to be within reach (1999: 153–4). This was operationalized, in the study presented below, into questions probing where help was depicted as coming from and in attention to reports portraying 'ordinary people' doing their bit – donating money to the Red Cross, helping out at relief centres, or simply coming together in public spaces to commune with others (constituting 'speech', which counts as a form of action in Boltanski's account).

One form of speech to which Boltanski devotes a good deal of thought is what he refers to as 'the topic of denunciation', which can be translated into the politicization of the catastrophe. Attention was thus paid in the study to the framing of tsunami reports in terms of the problems they dealt with. Were viewers invited to conclude that the suffering of the flood victims was due to an 'Act of God' (it was no one's fault the earthquake took place where it did; and it was because of heat rather than any human factor that disease spread as bodies decomposed) or that it was a result of human failings (the slow response of politicians or the lack of foresight of Asian governments that had neglected to install warning systems)?

While many before and after him have made a similar point, Boltanski nevertheless argues that 'the central problem confronted by a politics of pity is actually the *excess* of unfortunates. There are too many of them.' He is referring here not only to how many can be helped in reality, 'but also in the domain of representation: media space is not unlimited and cannot be entirely given over to showing misfortune' (1999: 155). Given that 230,000 people from dozens of countries perished within a few hours on the day of the tsunami, this is a relevant issue in the present analysis, and one question posed thus asked which countries were in focus in each report, while another asked whose version of events viewers were proffered. How much space did the unfortunates actually get? This question also served as an indicator of one tool used by journalists in their work of nourishing the imagination: inviting viewers to identify with the people in the news stories – or not.

Reporting the tsunami to national and global publics

To appreciate the media potential for community-building discussed above, and to further an understanding of television's potential as an agent of cosmopolitanization, it is necessary to entertain the possibility that performance varies from culture to culture, and that broadcasters addressing different sorts of publics may be nourishing different sorts of imaginations in different ways: this was set out in the preface as a central concern of this book. Consequently, a study of tsunami reporting was designed to include the contents of the main broadcasts of eight Europe-based channels over a period of fifteen days, beginning on 26 December 2004 – a total of 115 news broadcasts. To recapitulate from chapter 2: five of the channels targeted national audiences in Sweden, Spain, France, Germany and the UK, and three of the channels broadcast to global audiences as well as to viewers 'at home'.

The eight channels can be said to represent a cross-section of European broadcasting and are charged with the task of relaying news to viewers in large and small countries and in vaguely delineated global milieux. Table 4.1 shows how the material on which this chapter is based is distributed among the channels.

Beck argues that events and processes associated with such terms as '9/11' and 'the war on terrorism' create a global public by promoting a public awareness of risk (2006: 34). The first finding was that the tsunami, insofar as it was a risk brought to fruition, clearly provided the preconditions for such a global public. As figure 4.1 shows, evening newscasts aimed at audiences in Sweden, Spain, France, Germany and the UK and by BBC World, Deutsche Welle and EuroNews to global, or at least transnational, audiences gave saturation coverage to the catastrophe from the day the wave hit to the end of the following week. This applied to broadcasts in countries not directly affected, such as France, as well as countries such as Sweden, which literally went into a state of collective shock.

The results reported in figure 4.1 make it difficult to argue that global broadcasters were more active in promoting public

Table 4.1 The distribution of news items pertaining to the tsunami catastrophe in the main evening news programmes of eight broadcasters, 26 December 2004 – 9 January 2005[2]

	National Swedish	National Spanish	National French	National German	National British	Global British	Global German	Global European
Programmes n = 115	15	14	15	15	14	15	13	14
Tsunami items n = 925	15%	11%	24%	8%	8%	10%	16%	7%
Tsunami minutes n = 1,896	17%	9%	23%	9%	11%	14%	12%	5%

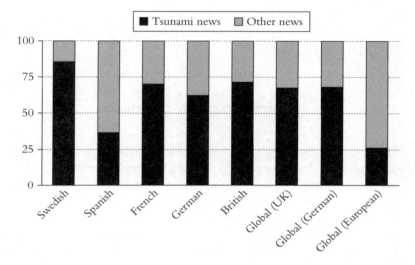

Figure 4.1 The proportion of broadcasts devoted to news about the tsunami, 26 December 2004 – 9

awareness of the catastrophe than national ones. The channels that devoted the highest percentage of their programmes to the catastrophe were all national. While Swedish television's top rating of 85.5 per cent can be explained by the fact that more Swedish lives were lost in the tsunami than in any other event since Napoleonic times, it does not apply to France, which was next in line, with 70 per cent. The similar figures noted for the two British channels (72 per cent of the BBC's news time and 67 per cent of BBC World's) and the two German channels (62 per cent and 68.5 per cent) suggest that the national origin of the broadcasts might have been as important as the audience (be it national or global) for which they were intended. With a little over 26 per cent of its programmes devoted to tsunami coverage, EuroNews – the only channel without a national base – was in a class of its own when it came to the modest quantity of contributions to a potential mobilization of the cosmopolitan imagination. At first glance, the Spanish news appears to display a tendency similar to EuroNews, but while the latter broadcast only sixty-one news items on the tsunami, *Telediario* had almost twice as many – 102 – which was more than any other broadcaster with the exception of Sweden,

France and Deutsche Welle. Obviously, different news formats are one explanation for the variation noted in figure 4.1. But they do not tell the whole story.

(Global) domestic politics?

One question the study addressed is how the 'map of tragedy' – the figures for the dead and missing from each country presented at the beginning of this chapter – was refracted on the 'maps of meaning' broadcast in the television news. This was explored partly by noting which countries were mentioned in each report (the results of this coding are too unwieldy to be presented here) and partly by noting which countries were the focus of a given report. The results of this analysis are presented in table 4.2.

As is evident here, the media maps do not correspond with those of the official agencies compiling statistics of death and destruction mentioned at the beginning of this chapter. Swedish and French television and Deutsche Welle focused considerably more often on Thailand than on Indonesia, despite the fact that ten times as many people died in the latter country. It is easy to conclude that this was on account of the presence of many Western holiday-makers in Thailand. This did not seem to have influenced British reporting, however, as both of the BBC channels concentrated on Indonesia more often than Thailand. Commonwealth ties and a large audience in India make the fact that BBC World had the highest proportion of reports centring on India something less than a surprise. While Sri Lanka was mentioned in sixteen reports on the Swedish channel, it was the focus of only 3.5 percent of the Swedish tsunami sample, a figure as low as for EuroNews. The others focused on this country, which suffered more casualties than any other after Indonesia, in a fifth to a third of broadcast time.

Countries in the afflicted region, however, were by no means the only ones featured in these news discourses. The reporting country itself was the focal point in a considerable number of reports broadcast on the national channels – in over half, or 55 per cent, of Swedish reports, in a quarter of German and in a fifth of

Table 4.2 Percentage of all items in which a given country is the focus of a news item about the tsunami in the eight programmes between 26 December 2004 and 9 January 2005

Country in focus	National Swedish n = 85	National Spanish n = 48	National French n = 148	National German n = 50	National British n = 57	Global British n = 67	Global German n = 60	Global European n = 32
Indonesia	13	42	15.5	22	26	31	16	37.5
Thailand	25	10	26	20	14	13	28	28
Sri Lanka	3	35	19	18	33	22	27	3
India	1	4	9	12	10.5	18	7	3
Reporting country	55	6	22	24	10.5	3	12	12.5
Other	3	2	7	2	6	10	10	15
Total	100	99	98.5	98	100	97	100	99

French ones. There are two exceptions to this pattern: Spain and Britain. Given the fact that no Spanish lives were lost, one could ask why Spain was the focus of as many as 3 per cent of reports at all. One answer applies to both France (which was spared in the tragedy) and Germany (which had many missing citizens at the time analysed here). It is that many reports dealt with measures taken by the government, the authorities and civil society in the reporting country to contribute to the rescue effort. This does not apply to Britain, as will be seen from tables 4.3 and 4.4. In any case, the figures reported in table 4.3 present the first indication that the assumption that the tsunami was an instance of global domestic politics may be problematic.

By definition, all of the 925 analysed news items were about the tsunami catastrophe. That event was, however, the point of departure for many different stories, framed in different ways. One thing coded for was consequently whether a given report dealt with a problem and, if so, what it was. All problems occurring in the reports were coded. A given report could thus deal with the problems of containing the spread of disease *and* lack of information. After being coded, the problems were aggregated into the overarching categories that appear in table 4.3.

Not surprisingly, perhaps, table 4.3 shows that most problems dealt with in the reporting of all eight broadcasters were what can be called 'human' ones, related to identifying the dead and saving the injured, controlling the spread of disease, and taking care of traumatized survivors. More interesting perhaps is the result which shows that the Swedish news had the highest proportion of reports dealing with a political problem, and that only the Swedish news had more political than aid-related problems. (The German news, however, had an equal proportion in these categories, and devoted the same attention to political problems as the two British channels.) Swedish coverage is also unique in that most of its 'political problem' reports dealt with a failing or problem related to the Swedish government rather than a foreign government, the EU or the UN.

It is worth noting that, while the Swedish foreign minister was severely criticized in the media for not having cancelled her theatre plans on 26 December, not a word was said on either BBC channel

Table 4.3 Percentage of tsunami reports on each channel in the sample in which a given problem/problem category is identified (no. = number of items in which a problem is mentioned)[3]

Problem	National Swedish n = 149	National Spanish n = 80	National French n = 115	National German n = 76	National British n = 66	Global British n = 103	Global German n = 115	Global Europe N = 55
Human	58	46	58	59	51.5	49.5	56	62
Political	19	10	6	14	12	13.5	9	7
Aid	13	32.5	26	14	13	32	26	22
Other	10	11.5	10	13	6	5	8.5	9
Total	100	100	100	100	82.5	100	99.5	100

about the fact that the British prime minister did not cancel his holiday, and returned to London only several days after the flood. This finding is in line with studies (e.g. Robertson 2000) which have shown that British television news stories contain more themes related to the inevitability of suffering and conflict, with Acts of God and/or inhuman forces figuring as the perpetrators of the misfortune. In their reports of the tsunami, BBC journalists told viewers at home that 'nature has taken everything', 'water is still the enemy', 'man's violence cannot compare to nature's' and that the afflicted were 'refugees not from war but from nature'. (Acts of God were not always a bad thing in some news discourses. French and Spanish reporting, for example, was replete with stories of 'miracles'.) In the Swedish texts analysed here, there were no Acts of God (or, in this case, 'Nature') or miracles; suffering was not inevitable and always had human agents. At times it seemed as though the Swedish foreign minister was personally responsible for the flood. In this respect, the Swedish reports resemble the Katrina coverage documented by Durham (2008), and constitute a challenge to the view that media and political institutions work in a consensual way at times of national crisis.

As outlined above, the ways in which action, or possible routes to action, are depicted are thought (by Boltanski at least) decisive in cultivating and maintaining the commitment of the spectator to alleviating the suffering of distant others. Such commitment could be a key element distinguishing the unconscious from the conscious cosmopolitan. One way of exploring the role journalists may have played in this sort of mobilization was to code for who was depicted as responsible for a solution to the problems featured in these reports. Answers could involve identifying whose business this was. Was the catastrophe something for elites, certain governments or organizations to take care of, or was it something that concerned other actors as well, including 'ordinary people' in safe, dry Europe, far from the tsunami's 'world of dread and fear'?

As can be seen from table 4.4, the answer varied from country to country and between national broadcasters, on the one hand, and global broadcasters, on the other. Sweden and Britain can be said to represent the two extremes. At the one extreme the Swedish news identified its own government as responsible for a

Table 4.4 Responsibility for solving the problems depicted in tsunami reports: the percentage of all actors identified by each broadcaster (n = number of items in which a given actor is identified as responsible for a solution to a tsunami-related problem)[4]

Problem-solvers	National Swedish n = 71	National Spanish n = 11	National French n = 46	National German n = 15	National British n = 12	Global British n = 9	Global German n = 27	Global European n = 27
Own country	45	33	11	27	8	0	15	0
Other country	8	18	11	20	25	11	22	33
World community	11	36	17	27	50	55	26	18.5
NGOs	17	9	41	0	8	33	15	33
Ordinary people	11	0	15	27	0	0	11	7
Other	7	3	4	0	8	0	11	8
Total	99	99	99	101	99	99	100	99.5

solution in 45 per cent of the items in which responsibility occurs. This is perhaps not surprising, given the frequency of problems associated with a failing on the part of that government. At the other extreme, the British domestic broadcaster identified other governments or the world community as responsible for a solution in 75 per cent of such items, as did BBC World in 66 per cent.

This can be interpreted in different ways, either as indicating that it was up to those other than Britain to solve the problems, or that the world was pulling together on this matter. In the Spanish, French and German news there is a more even distribution of items identifying their own governments as having responsibility and those suggesting it was the business of the world community. In the case of the Swedish news, 'ordinary people' (for want of a better term) accounted for as large a proportion of items as the world community – the same proportion as in the German news – while there were none at all mentioned by either British broadcaster. Similarly noticeable in French reporting is the attention given to NGOs and aid workers when responsibility for solutions is in focus.

The tsunami stories were only partly about death and destruction. They had as much, if not more, to do with the rescue and reconstruction effort, which involved actors other than the afflicted. Where, then, is help depicted as coming from? Who demonstrates a commitment to action in these reports?

There are two features of table 4.5 to note in particular. The first is that news reports represented a wide variety of actors, from all over the world, coming together to help the victims of the tsunami. This involved international elites and abstractions such as the UN, the EU, the 'world community' and often simply 'the world', and in every channel (except EuroNews) included the government of the reporting country 10 to 30 per cent of the time. NGOs were mentioned – especially in the French, Spanish and global channels – and the people working for them, be they doctors, nurses or other volunteers. Priests, rabbis, Muslim leaders, members of the business community, celebrities and prisoners were also represented. Many of these actors and organizations were based in the reporting country. In German and French domestic broadcasts, help was depicted as coming from the reporting country in about half of the items dealing with assistance.

Table 4.5 Percentage of tsunami reports in each channel in which a given actor/type of actor is mentioned as a source of assistance (n = number of items in which an actor is depicted as the origin of help)[5]

Actor	National Swedish n = 41	National Spanish n = 41	National French n = 117	National German n = 50	National British n = 34	Global British n = 37	Global German n = 85	Global European n = 39
Own country	19.5	27	14	38	29	16	26	0
Afflicted country	0	5	2	6	12	5	2	5
World community	7	22	3	18	12	35	22	49
NGOs	7	12	20.5	6	9	16	15	20.5
Aid workers	14	17	36	10	9	13.5	16	18
Ordinary people	41	17	16	18	23	11	8	2.5
Other	10	0	8.5	4	6	3	9	5
Total	98.5	100	100	100	100	99.5	98	100

Many of these items were characterized by a tone of eagerness to show both what was being done to help and the specific contribution made by the reporting country, be it the government or its inhabitants. The Spanish news, for example, kept reminding viewers not only that the government was doing everything it could to help, but also that Spanish aid workers were in the thick of relief efforts. A report on 2 January portrayed a Spanish nurse, Sella, saving people in Phuket and interviewed her worried but proud mother. Prime Minister Zapatero's words about Spanish 'solidarity' recurred in *Telediario*'s discourse throughout the week.

The second feature of table 4.5 to note is that 'ordinary people' were prominent in the reports of all the national channels (and in Sweden in particular), while they played a much more insignificant role in all three global channels. Reports of various aspects of the relief effort often began with a line mentioning how 'you and I' were doing our bit – donating money to the Red Cross, helping out at relief centres, or simply coming together in public spaces to commune with others (which would constitute 'speech', a form of action in Boltanski's account).

In one BBC World report, viewers were told that more than half of the tourists who died in Thailand were thought to have come from Scandinavia, and that 3,500 Swedes were still missing. 'But the collections are for their Thai hosts and companions in grief', said the reporter, to views of a well-filled Swedish cathedral, before moving on to images of similar sentiments in an Italian piazza.[6] In one Swedish broadcast, the newsreader told viewers that 'Up to 5 million people are in urgent need of aid after the catastrophe, and the willingness of the Swedish people to help out knows no limits. In one and a half days the Red Cross has collected more than five times the amount it usually does in a year, and new spontaneous collections start all the time.' One woman filmed giving money on a snowy Stockholm street explained: 'It is very important to feel involved. It feels very petty to be here in Sweden when things like this are happening.'

In her study of the Bhopal disaster, Wilkins found that media reports portrayed individuals as powerless and concluded that such portrayals hindered the development of community (1989: 33). A somewhat different picture emerges here. Audience surveys after

Bhopal said that fewer than 33 per cent had retained a specific image of the tragedy (ibid.: 28). An intriguing question (which unfortunately cannot be answered here) is whether media reports of a different tragedy, with depictions of individuals as actors and not just helpless victims or passive spectators, would have proved more memorable.

Given that the global public space created by the tsunami discourse was populated by such a broad spectrum of actors, it is instructive to see whose version of events viewers were offered by the different broadcasters. How distant was the suffering? This question also served as an indicator of one tool used by journalists in their work of nourishing the imagination: inviting viewers to identify with the people in the news stories. Table 4.6 shows the distribution of news items in which different sorts of actors were interviewed – i.e. appeared speaking 'in their own words'. Of interest here was whether it was political elites (widely considered to populate the ranks of the world's cosmopolitans) or more ordinary people (who, Lewis et al. (2005) tell us, tend to be given the role of extras if they are portrayed at all) who served as the 'primary definers' of the crisis. The results confirm one of the patterns that emerged in table 4.5: that, with the exception of Deutsche Welle, 'ordinary people' figured more largely in the reports of the national broadcasters than in those of the global ones. Those who figured most prominently in every channel, however, were the afflicted – people who had experienced the flood or who had lost a loved one. After them came civil society actors, aid workers and experts. Elites had to share the stage with figures more recognizable from everyday life, people easier to relate to or identify with, and even (to mix the metaphor further) take a back seat to them.

Reflexivity in tsunami narratives

A recurrent theme in tsunami reports was that 'the world' was joining together to respond to the catastrophe, which can be said to reflect an awareness of global interdependence. In the French

Table 4.6 Distribution of actors: figures indicate the percentage of all items in which a given category of actor is quoted (n = number of items in which one or more actors from a given category speaks in their own words)

Who speaks?	National Swedish n = 185	National Spanish n = 51	National French n = 268	National German n = 98	National British n = 95	Global British n = 97	Global German n = 183	Global European n = 38
Afflicted person	20	29	33	29	46	39	17	16
Ordinary person	8	6	11	3	3	0	5	0
NGO actor	18	39	27	27	22	21	21	18
Own official	21	6	4	14	1	4	9	0
Other official	5	12	5	16	18	26	37	55
Other	26	8	20	10	9	9	11	11
Total	98	100	100	99	99	99	100	100

programme of 7 January, for example, the newsreader noted that the world had never shown such solidarity: 'we are suddenly all equal, with no difference between nationalities'. German viewers of *Heute* were told on 29 December that 'the catastrophe shows we live in one world'. This in fact echoed official German discourse, as President Köhler said in a speech on 30 December that the lesson of the tsunami was that 'we have to think of the world as one world', and both he and Chancellor Schröder called for a 'domestic policy for the world'. Deutsche Welle reported Schröder the following day as saying that he wanted people to feel responsible for their fellow humans on the other side of the earth, with each individual country giving aid to another country, each province to another province in another part of the world, each city to another city and each village to another village.

The material analysed here contains examples of a reflexive awareness in stories taking a macro-view (typically in the global broadcasters) and those zooming in on individuals (often in the national sample). A report in BBC World on 2 January, for example, considered how the world's faiths responded to the challenge of explaining the suffering of those afflicted by the tsunami. The reporter built a discursive bridge between the global and the local by visiting Hindu, Buddhist, Muslim and Christian places of worship in London, where people were seen praying in the background for the souls and lost lives of people in faraway Asia: 'Suffering was the unnoticed fact of everyday life for millions of people before the disaster in Asia. The tsunami just brought more of it on an unimaginable scale. But it's focused attention as never before on where tragedy comes from and why people must suffer it.'

From the level of the world's religions to that of the individual survivor: a man who, together with his partner and their two children, survived the catastrophe was the central figure in a story on the Swedish news three days after the flood. Back home in front of his Christmas tree, Tony Eklund said he was convinced he owed his life to local Thais, who helped his family and twenty other tourists escape up to the mountains. He spoke of one man in a little mountain village in particular, relating how the Thai had made food for the stranded tourists out of nothing, on a camping stove, without any thought for himself or his own loved ones. 'I am so deeply grateful', said the Swede. 'I can't . . . it's impossible to understand how a nation can be so generous in such a situation.' To show his gratitude, he had begun collecting donations for the little mountain village the day after his return: 'They gave us everything they had when we were in need. And now we're back in Sweden where we have an incredible overabundance. And they have nothing left.' Even if Tony said he had difficulty fathoming the generosity of the Thai villagers, he would seem to have been aware, on some level, that their fates became interconnected on 26 December, or, as Beck would put it, that the familiar distinctions between internal and external, us and them, needed some rethinking.

As mentioned earlier, Becker (1995) maintains that a 'peak moment' in a media event can be used by television cameras to summarize or condense its meaning, and that such action fosters the reflexivity on which community depends. One such moment occurred on 5 January 2005, when Europeans observed three minutes of silence to honour the tsunami victims. At this point, more than any other in this mediated event, viewers became actors as well as spectators, at least in some media cultures.

The three channels broadcasting to global audiences simply reported the fact of the silent tribute, although EuroNews did draw a parallel with 9/11 and the Madrid bombings. The nationals made more of it, in dramatic and rather moving reports. 'At 12 o'clock today', said the anchor in Stockholm, 'Sweden and Europe stood still.' The report, which began by saying that 'time stood still' on town squares, railway stations and workplaces, emphasized the stillness by broadcasting images of people pausing in such public spaces, with furrowed brows or tears streaming down their cheeks, for a minute, without the voice of any newsreader or reporter to break the silence. The BBC *Ten O'Clock News* referred to similar spaces in a report about 'a country and continent united in remembrance'. Opening with the most British symbol of all, Big Ben, sounding a death toll, viewers were told: 'It happened half a world away, yet has touched the lives of people everywhere. And at midday, Britain paused to reflect.'

Disturbing routines

'Every now and then', writes Cottle (2006: 54), 'exceptional, high-profile media phenomena breach normal conventions, disturb routines of news reporting and culturally reverberate throughout society.' The media in general, and television in particular, played an extraordinary role in the days following the tsunami. It is easy to find evidence to support an argument that broadcasters forged a 'democratic feeling community'. The connectivity they engendered was not just, or not necessarily, political or civic, but served what Becker (1995: 631) has referred to as a religious function. This happened on a discursive as well as a metaphysical level. Playing a role previously accorded to churches, the television news offered a site for people to congregate – to come, sit, reflect on the vulnerability of human life, and gain succour from knowing that others were communing in the same space of the emotional imagination, at the same (real) time.

To what extent can responses to the catastrophe, seen through the 925 news reports analysed here, be thought to constitute an instance of 'global domestic politics'? Did people 'experience themselves as parts of a fragmented, endangered civilization and civil society characterized by the simultaneity of events and of knowledge of this simultaneity all over the world' (Beck 2006: 42)? Strictly speaking, such questions cannot be answered on the basis of textual analysis alone, but it can be argued that a meta-narrative of a global public can be traced in all the eight channels – a narrative of a world mourning and acting together, or at least watching together. Reporting both made the suffering of distant others tangible and provided a commentary on what spectators should be experiencing and doing: in this way, television reporters supplied a reflexive dimension, and the narratives they produced can be thought to have promoted an active cosmopolitan outlook, if only for a moment – or only at times, or in certain contexts.

At other times, and in other contexts, the tsunami was not a story of distant suffering at all, but rather of suffering directly experienced: a matter of domestic politics, without the 'global' adjective. This was the case with a good deal of Swedish reporting,

for example, but also Spanish and French. The two British broadcasters are the exception here. Be that as it may, one clear finding,
and one certainly worth reflecting upon, is that the global broadcasters did not have more to contribute to the mobilizing of the
imagination than the national ones, and in the case of EuroNews
had considerably less. While Swedish, British, French and German
news devoted more than half of their broadcast time (and in some
cases up to three-quarters) to the tsunami, EuroNews (the only
non-nationally based channel in the study) devoted only a quarter
of its news space to the catastrophe.

More important than the amount of space, however, is how it
was used – how the imaginations of viewers were nourished. In
Beck's vision of cosmopolitanism, political action among strangers takes place in ways that are familiar from national settings.
The results presented here suggest that this may be because it is in
national settings that cosmopolitan sentiments are fostered, not least
in what Durham (2008) calls 'media ritual in catastrophic time'. At
peak moments such as the silent tribute of 5 January, it was possible to observe national broadcasters mobilizing cosmopolitanism
in an active, reflexive form. Viewers literally saw themselves doing
what Boltanski theorized – imagining the suffering of others. The
question is whether the moment was capable of being 'fleshed out'
and the cosmopolitan sentiments to which it gave rise applied to
other situations.

Although it yields many insights into cosmopolitan empathy,
it is not clear what lessons the tsunami coverage teaches us when
it comes to a more enduring relation between the media and cosmopolitanism. The tsunami was only the first of several natural
disasters to blight 2005, as hurricane Katrina ravaged the Americas
later in the year, and a humanitarian crisis caused by the earthquake in Pakistan followed closely on its heels. Neither they nor
the natural catastrophes in Burma and China in 2008 received the
saturation coverage that the tsunami did, but they were extensively
reported. The outpouring of common purpose, however, was not
repeated: active cosmopolitanism apparently reverted to its latent
mode. When it came to the tsunami, Band Aid can be paraphrased:
'Tonight, God help us, it's us as well as them'. European publics
could imagine themselves in this situation, as they perhaps could

not imagine themselves in a New Orleans slum, a refugee camp in Kashmir, or the rubble of a collapsed tower block in Sichuan. After the emotional drain of the tsunami, it could also be that 'the discourse of global compassion' (Höijer 2004) gave way to 'compassion fatigue' (Moeller 1999). The lessons to be learned from this need not be about cynical, self-interested audiences – the triumph of communitarianism over humanitarianism, in Boltanski's terms. It could simply be that claims about the power of mediated messages, as compared to the impressions gleaned from lived experience, may be subject to exaggeration, and that the role of television in 'global domestic politics' needs to be problematized and subjected to more empirical study.

5

Old Wars in News Programmes:
Cosmopolitanism, Media and Memory

'People forget about World War II, the things they did to people', the man in the bar told the journalist. 'They don't show those pictures.' It was May 2004, and the BBC reporter was interviewing inhabitants of the West Virginian town that had achieved infamy overnight with the publication of photographs showing a local woman, Lynndie England, humiliating Iraqi prisoners of war in Abu Ghraib.

To most viewers, the assertion that no one had been shown pictures of 'what they did to people' in the Second World War would be as easy to swallow as the claim made in the aftermath of the Iraq intervention by Lynndie's family and neighbours that she had been framed. For generations, people the world over have been on the receiving end of lessons at school, books on coffee tables, films at the cinema and documentaries on television about the horrors of twentieth-century wars. And yet the man in the small American town had a point. Like individuals, societies are selective about what they forget and how they interpret what is remembered.

This is an insight which scholars from a variety of disciplines have been sharing with their readers for quite some time, in connection with research on nationalism, collective identity, and what has come to be known as 'the discursive construction of history'

(Heer et al. 2008; see also Ashuri 2006; Baer 2001; Barthes 1993; Bell 2007; Bhabha 1990; Birkvad 2000; Calabrese 2007; Chapman 2007; Dayan and Katz 1992; De Leeuw 2007; Dhoest 2007; Ebbrecht 2007; Kitzinger 2000; Robertson 2000; Sturken 1997; Thompson 1995; Thompson 1997; Wood 1991). Encountering glaring attempts to reconfigure the past in the context of contemporary world affairs nevertheless provides cause for reflection.

Smith (1990) has famously argued that specific, historical cultures possess 'strong emotional connotations for those who share in the particular culture' and that traditions will only survive and flourish as part of the repertoire of national culture. Revived traditions may be successful, insofar as they draw on older ones, the memories of which remain alive: they 'were only able to flourish because they could be presented, and were accepted, as continuous with a valued past'. It might be possible to package imagery and diffuse it around the world, Smith concedes, but he does not accept that such images retain their power to move and inspire people long divided by history and culture. Images reflect collective identities, they do not form them. Smith is sceptical about the possibility of shared memories and a sense of common destiny existing beyond the nation, for, unlike national cultures, cosmopolitan culture fails to relate to historical identity and is 'essentially memoryless' (1990: 178–9).

However, Smith is not very helpful in explaining why traditions can be revived in a national setting but not in the context of a wider community. National cultures, he maintains, are particular and timebound. Could the same not be said of the international community at a particular historical juncture – for example, at a time when a historical war, which had divided a continent within living memory, was being revisited and the overcoming of those historical divisions celebrated?

As Ashuri (2006) points out, the media form one of the main mnemonic sites in contemporary society. She and others have written about how the media contribute to the sense of belonging to a larger collectivity by forging imagined social relationships that extend across time as well as space (Frosch and Wolfsfeld 2006; Schudson 1994; Thompson 1995). Levy and Sznaider (2002) and Holton (2009) write specifically of 'cosmopolitan memory', which is cultural and lives on after the people who experienced a particular formative event. They have the Holocaust in mind. This chapter focuses on a different watershed in the same war. It is about reports of the commemoration of the Normandy invasion and what they may mean for cosmopolitan understandings – or their opposite – of the present.

The concern of chapter 2 could be said to have been with mediated spatial relations, although this was not a conscious research strategy. Despite pressing contemporary problems and issues, preliminary coding established that a significant amount of airtime was devoted to historical events, and closer reading, with attention to narrative themes, indicated that many of these reports were situated in what could be considered a discourse of European identity-formation. It was as if temporality was tugging on my sleeve and pointing insistently in a direction different from that mapped out in the study design. The purpose of this chapter is to make sense of the invocation of the old in the new(s) by comparing reporting of the anniversary of the Normandy invasion and reflecting on what such news stories seem to be saying about the world six decades on. What do they entail for the study of cosmopolitanism?

Cosmopolitanism and mediated historicity

As should by now be clear, my ambition in analysing television news has not been to assess the accuracy of reports or the likelihood or otherwise of viewers becoming well-informed citizens by watching the news on a regular basis. The interest has been to see whether those viewers have been invited (for whatever reason) to think of themselves as members of a society extending across national borders, and perhaps even to feel that they have something in common with people elsewhere. It has also been suggested that a 'narrative understanding' is key to this – a conception of how the different parts of the world cohere and what the relation of the individual citizen is to that world and the people in it.

In his influential study of the media and modernity, John Thompson draws heavily on hermeneutics, not least the insight that, when people take hold of messages and incorporate them into their lives on a routine basis, they 'are implicitly involved in constructing a sense of self, a sense of who we are and where we are situated in space and time' (Thompson 1995: 43). Throughout his book, he emphasizes the importance of the symbolic dimension of media messages.

Taking a historical approach, Thompson argues that, from handwritten Bibles, through print, to the McLuhanesque 'cool' medium of television, the media have played a central role in forming people's understanding of the world beyond their immediate experiences. 'Our sense of the past,' he writes, 'and our sense of the ways in which the past impinges on us today, has become increasingly dependent on an ever expanding reservoir of mediated symbolic forms.' He refers to this phenomenon as 'mediated historicity' (Thompson 1995: 34). The media alter our sense of place and of the past, which in turn affects our feeling of belonging to different groups and communities. Feelings of belonging underlie our actions and come from the experience of sharing a common history. Mediated symbolic forms are altering this experience, according to this argument, for,

> as our sense of the past becomes increasingly dependent on mediated symbolic forms, and as our sense of the world and our place within it becomes increasingly nourished by media products, so too our sense of the groups and communities with which we share a common fate is altered: we feel ourselves to belong to groups and communities which are constituted in part through the media. (Thompson 1995: 35)

Thompson takes issue with fellow sociologists who consider tradition (i.e. anything which is transmitted or handed down from previous generations) to be a thing of the past. It is not something we have left behind, he maintains, but something that has become transformed, not least by the media. It has, in his account, four aspects. The first is hermeneutic. Seen from this perspective, tradition consists of a set of background assumptions that are taken for granted, passed on from one generation to the next, and serve as an interpretive framework for understanding the world (Thompson 1995: 184). The second aspect is normative, by which Thompson means that sets of assumptions and patterns of action handed down from the past function as normative guides for actions and beliefs in the present. Drawing on Weber, Thompson understands the third aspect of tradition – legitimation – to be that which sustains power and authority. Like Weber, Thompson insists that this renders tradition political. The fourth aspect of tradition has to do with identity, which involves a sense both of self and of the collective: 'it is a sense of belonging, a sense of being part of a social group which has a history of its own and a collective fate' (ibid.: 186).

The collection of reports summarized below form a striking instance of mediated historicity. Considering them as such, however – in the singular, as the collective product of an entity called 'the media' – would be to miss the point. What is interesting is to see how different television discourses about the tradition of 'the longest day' highlight different aspects of the event.

While Thompson writes about the media in general, it has been suggested in previous chapters that television news in particular is a rich source of recurrent narratives that keep cultural memories and shared understandings alive. There is reason, it has been argued, to turn to news reports as sites for the rehearsal of historical and cultural themes that give meaning to and make sense of an ever changing, and often turbulent, political environment.

In this chapter, news narratives from all the channels on which this book is based (with the exception of the Spanish and French programmes that made a guest appearance in chapter 4) will be presented in such a way that the various components of the Chatman/Labov anatomy are more readily apparent. A recapitulation of the method involved, and elucidation of some operationalizations not yet presented, is thus in order.

After analysing the superficial features of the 285 programmes which featured in chapter 2, narrative analysis sought to compare their interpretive frameworks of 'common, cultural references and thematic codes, incarnated in master or model narratives' (Birkvad 2000: 295). Each news item of a minute or more in length that in some way related to the outside world or showed a connection between the reporting country and that world was coded, with attention paid to story (*histoire*) and discourse (*discours*). Consideration was given to the six common elements of story structure outlined in chapter 1: the abstract (the anchor's lead-in), the orientation (established by asking what was happening, when, where and to whom); the complicating action; the evaluation (coded as whether the meaning of the action is commented on and, if so, what it is); the resolution (i.e. what finally happened); and the coda, which returns the perspective to the present (operationalized as the exchange between the reporter on site and the anchor in the newsroom). Analysing the *histoire* involved establishing what story was being told.

Analysing the *discours* meant documenting *how* the story was told. Questions posed to the news texts included: From which vantage point does the narrative unfold? Is it possible to identify with any of the central actors and, if so, are they elites or ordinary people? What are their traits? What metaphors are used? What symbolism is deployed?

What follows is a fruit salad with some of these findings thrown in. It is a medley of some of the similarities and differences between the reports in the six different channels, and is served with excerpts of individual reports which provide particularly clear illustrations of television news as a site of tradition – framing and redefining the global environment.

Where history is fashioned

While a variety of historical events were invoked as frames for unfolding current affairs throughout the period here, the live broadcast of the sixtieth anniversary of D-Day serves as the focal point for the following discussion. Table 5.1 shows how the material on which this chapter is based was distributed.

D-Day is widely acknowledged to have been the turning point of the Second World War. On 6 June 1944, about 3.5 million Allied troops crossed the channel from England to Normandy with the task of driving the Nazis out of France. The majority of the troops came from the US, the UK and Canada, but soldiers

Table 5.1 Distribution of items mentioning the anniversary of D-Day in the main evening news programmes of six broadcasters, 26 April – 13 June 2004

	BBC	*Heute*	*Rapport*	BBC World	*Deutsche-Welle*	Euro-News	Total
Total no. of items in sample	420	610	705	548	571	536	3,390
No. of D–Day items	11	7	3	10	9	20	60
No. of D–Day minutes	37	15	9	30	19	80	190

from Australia and New Zealand, Czechoslovakia and Poland, Belgium, France, the Netherlands and Greece also took part. They succeeded in their objective, but suffered an estimated 10,000 casualties, including 2,500 dead. The number of German casualties has never been established, but is thought to have been at least 4,000 and perhaps as many as 9,000. The Normandy invasion took place two days after the Americans marched victoriously into Rome and only a few weeks after the protracted Battle of Montecassino finally ended, leaving 54,000 Allied and 20,000 German casualties in its wake. The period from which the sample was drawn thus contained some significant anniversaries. At the same time, a year after US President Bush had proclaimed the 'liberation' of Iraq, both occupying forces and civilians continued to die in Fallujah, Najaf and Baghdad on a daily basis. Finally, as mentioned earlier, former enemies had just become partners in the newly enlarged European Union. Against this backdrop, the following pages sketch how the world in general, and the conflicts of 1944 in particular, were represented in the reports of the six broadcasters.

BBC Ten O'Clock News

In the weeks studied here, the war in Iraq was a constant concern in BBC newscasts, in which it had to do with domestic politics,

with bilateral US–UK relations and, to a lesser degree, with international politics. In reports of war commemorations and President
Bush's trip to Europe to take part in these, however, Iraq became
an American problem. At the end of May, a memorial ceremony
in the US was the topic of one story in which parallels were
drawn between the two wars. The anchor introduced the report
by telling viewers that the war in Iraq continued to dominate US
domestic politics, before handing over to the reporter on site at
the memorial ceremony in Washington. The piece opened to the
sound of a choir singing 'God Bless America' and a close-up shot
of veterans, referred to in the voiceover as 'the greatest generation'. The camera then cut to a shot of younger soldiers in the
crowd, as the reporter explained that the mantle had now fallen
to a younger generation fighting a very different and unpopular
war. In what could be called the 'complicating action' in narrative
analysis, President Bush was given a sound bite, in which he drew a
positive parallel between the conflict in the 1940s and Iraq. 'In the
history books the Second World War can appear as a series of crises
and conflicts, following an inevitable course', Bush said, going on
to argue that, on the day the war began and in the hard days that
followed, the outcome was far from certain. The public was presumably meant to understand that, just as things worked out in the
Second World War, so they would in Iraq. Contradicting the spin,
veterans on site expressed their scepticism, and in the resolution
(which returns to the main theme of the narrative) the reporter
explained to British viewers: 'At a time when the nation remem-
bers the veterans of battles past, thoughts also turn to Iraq. And
for many, the contrasts are stark. Gone are the grand alliances and
moral clarity of yesteryear. And in their place are growing doubts
about the battle at hand.' [1]

A few days later, the *Ten O'Clock News* began a series of reports
to mark the sixtieth anniversary of D-Day. They had their own
signature, with a stylized picture of a gun, and theme music, highly
reminiscent of Elgar's 'Nimrod', the heroic hunter theme from
the *Enigma Variations*. The first report followed two veterans, one
British and one German, who were returning to the Normandy
beaches where they had fought each other six decades previously.
The reporter, Charles Wheeler, had himself been at the landing as

Plate 5.1   The BBC's Charles Wheeler on the beach at Normandy

a Royal Marine and took an active part in telling the story. It began with black-and-white archive footage of soldiers heading into the battle, with the voices of the British veteran recounting what had happened to him. The German, speaking impeccable English, was subsequently introduced in the same way, with a sepia-toned picture of a young soldier superimposed on a battle scene and accompanied by the voice of the old man he had become. After listening to Reg Clark and Bruno Lieblich, Wheeler turned to the camera, looked directly at viewers, and explained what it was like on the beach back then, gesturing for emphasis and switching from the past tense to an uncharacteristically direct form of audience address: 'You cross the beach if you're lucky to be still alive, and what you've got to do now is get up that slope with enemy fire coming from the right and the left and dead ahead and mortars going off all round you . . .' (see plate 5.1).

The report is a long one – almost five minutes – and a good deal of time is spent recounting the details of the military operation. Towards the end of the narrative, Bruno recounts his thoughts upon surrendering to the Allies. Reg asks him whether he was afraid they might shoot. 'Not really', replies Bruno. 'I thought you were decent people like me, you know?' They laugh. 'Hoping', he adds, as the camera pans on the sun setting on the sea: 'I was hoping they were decent like me!' In the resolution of this particular narrative, Wheeler explains that, after three years in prisoner of war camps in the UK and the US, the erstwhile German soldier married an English woman and 'brought up a British family'. The Englishman, Reg, stayed in the army for thirty-five years and married a German girl.[2]

This coda was the first and last time a BBC account of the Normandy invasion contained a cosmopolitan message, albeit understated. And the story itself is about military adventure, about exciting encounters in the past, rather than their aftermath. Subsequent reports, broadcast as the anniversary of D-Day approached, had even more to do with British derring-do. They emphasized the bravery of the Allied soldiers of 1944 and the success of their mission. That is not to say that they were 'stiff upper lip' in tone. They also gave considerable scope to the emotions, both those of the men who made the journey back to Normandy and those of the audience that were played upon.

One such report featured the elderly actor Richard Todd, who had fought in the battle of Pegasus Bridge and returned twenty years later to star in a film about it, *The Longest Day*. Resorting again to black-and-white newsreels and peppering the narrative with excerpts from the movie, the reporter and Todd reconstructed the landing together. Heavy casualties were sustained by the airborne forces, acknowledges the reporter, 'but they hung on to their objectives. And that success can't be overstated.' Todd speaks of seeing chaps around him being killed, and has to stop, choking on his tears. 'Difficult. Difficult to epitomize', he manages, unable to say more. The report cuts diplomatically at this point to an excerpt from *The Longest Day*, complete with stirring soundtrack, in which Todd is very much in control of both himself and the situation. At the end, the old actor says that D-Day was the making of him, but asks, as the camera pans row upon row of gravestones in a nearby military ceremony, 'Why do people have to go on bringing bloodshed and war? Come and look at Normandy. We wouldn't want to do this all over again.'

The next day, the BBC began to broadcast live from Normandy. Apart from the anchor in London, a correspondent played the role of secondary anchor in Arromanches, orchestrating the accounts of the other reporters on site. Viewers were told that the famous beaches had been called into service again, not to liberate Europe, but so that subsequent generations could honour those who did. 'It is the acknowledgement of an immeasurable debt', explained the Normandy anchor. The pluckiness of the old British vets was emphasized again in this broadcast. One of them, Reginald Smith, tells a reporter: 'The hospital people said, "You shouldn't be going because you won't come back". I said, "You think I'm going to pop it while I'm here?" I said, "I don't give a damn", because I says they can cremate me and put me with some of me mates . . .'

The BBC reports all concern 'then', rather than 'now'. These news stories are closed texts (a term used to refer to texts that allow only one interpretation, that do not leave it to the viewer or reader to draw their own conclusions). The message was that taking up arms in defence of liberty and crossing the sea to free fellow humans from oppressors is noble, heroic, and at times the only option. As the camera panned yet again on the sun rising over the sea, a third reporter, referring to the Normandy beaches, said:

> They have the power reserved for places where history was fashioned. Despite the passing of the years, they can never be considered just as beaches. For on these strips of Normandy coastline occurred events which have touched the lives of every one of us. Not far from the beaches are the cemeteries. The largest, overlooking the sea, is where nearly 10,000 Americans are buried – a reminder of the time when the new world came to the assistance of the old and sent so many of its young soldiers to die.

Although by this point the viewer could be forgiven for wondering whether Basil Fawlty was lurking behind a sand dune, admonishing reporters not to mention the (Iraq) war, the association was presumably reasonably clear to most.

As mentioned above, many of these reports gave uncharacteristic scope for emotions. As one retired officer, who was interviewed on the crossing from Portsmouth, spoke of comrades in arms who had died, tears streamed down his cheeks: 'I hope that some day people will think, well, it was worth it. I think it was worth it.

Sure it was worth it. In fact I know it was worth it, I know it was.' Another soldier is quoted as saying that, if you come to Normandy and don't weep, then it is no place for you. 'And that's the thing about D-Day', concludes the reporter in what narrativists would call the coda. 'Even after sixty years, its memories still bring tears to the eyes of those who were there.' Because, we are told, what happened on D-Day still matters.[3] By the time the anniversary itself was celebrated, on 6 June, the quiet heroism of the old British soldiers and the martyrdom of their fallen comrades had emerged as the BBC leitmotif. The evaluation of the overarching narrative (in which the meaning of the event is commented on) emerges clearly in the final debriefing between the anchor in London and a reporter on the site of the commemoration.

> *Reporter:* And on a day of extraordinary dignity, [. . .] the generation of the Normandy landings has gathered one last time to take a quiet, unassuming pride in who they are and what they gave.
> *Anchor:* There can never have been a gathering with more to be proud about.
> *Reporter:* That's right. The atmosphere here [. . .] is strangely under-stated. This is not a generation that shouts its achievements from the rooftops. But that said, there is a sort of steely determination to remind the world that this was a generation that was defined by the way it responded to the crisis, and they're here sixty years on to say, "This is what we did", and quietly, and deservedly, "We're quite proud of it".

If the BBC told British viewers that their veterans deserved to be proud of what they had done, what did the German newsroom have to say to its audience? How did the world in general, and D-Day in particular, look from the vantage point of the nation that had suffered such a historic defeat?

Heute

The German domestic broadcaster made sure its viewers under-stood this was a political event and not just about history. Both the anchor and reporters referred in several broadcasts to 'symbolic politics' taking place on the site of the commemoration. Where the British viewer may well have formed the impression that it was American and British troops that liberated France, the German programme made it clear that fourteen nations had taken part in the invasion – an invasion 'that was the beginning of the liberation of Europe from the terror of Hitler'. Not surprisingly, it drew attention to the fact that a German chancellor had been invited to attend the ceremony for the first time, something in which the BBC had shown little interest.

En route to Normandy, *Heute* documented Bush's stopover in Rome. German viewers could see how the US president was met by protesters playing dead on the streets of the capital and the sight of statues covered with the black masks reminiscent of an Abu Ghraib icon, as well as by a pontiff who criticized the US for its actions in Iraq. A contemporary street scene, with the flashing blue light of a police car in the foreground, was juxtaposed with black-and-white footage of Italians on the same street cheering the entry of US soldiers into Rome sixty years earlier. Although not articulated, the message seemed to be that liberating a country was no longer what it used to be.

The following day, the *Heute* anchor told viewers that Europe and America would be looking at Normandy that weekend, 'for, exactly sixty years ago, the Allied landing marked the beginning of the victory over Nazi Germany. Or, as Chancellor Schröder said: it was a victory for Germany.' As the BBC had done (and the other four channels would also do), the *Heute* newsroom rehearsed the military and historical details of the invasion with the help of black-and-white period footage. Interestingly, the voiceover referred to 'the Germans', as if they were some other people than the domestic audience watching the programme. There was a shot of a graveyard not seen in other coverage – a cemetery where German soldiers were buried – but the reporter explained that Schröder would not be there on the anniversary. He would be commemorating German soldiers, but at the cemetery where Germans were buried with soldiers of other nationalities. A German veteran of the Wehrmacht was interviewed and said of Schröder: 'I get the feeling he wanted to show that times have changed, that it's different now, that we Germans finally belong here.'

In a somewhat ironical tone, the report focused on younger people, who had not been born when the landings took place, but who had dressed up in period costumes for the commemoration and were enthusiastically taking part in the re-enactment of D-Day. These re-enactments were juxtaposed with what the reporter called the 'real politics taking place in France', where Bush was seeking support for the new Iraq resolution. The following day, this was referred to again. 'There was no place today for French–US disagreements', said the reporter. 'Today it was all about the community of values that binds the countries together.'

The D-Day commemoration topped the German broadcast on 6 June. In this account, unity and reconciliation were the key concepts. More than previous ones, said the anchor, this anniversary was taking place 'in the spirit of new partnerships'. Unified, the Russian president and the German chancellor joined with the usual celebrants in honouring the 10,000 who had died on D-Day. While the BBC had cast the dead as heroes, the German programme referred to them as victims. The first story of the day opened to the sound of church bells ringing and the voice of the correspondent saying that, 'As the sun rises today, the world is a different one, a better one, than it was sixty years ago [. . .] War in Europe is in the past.'

The speeches of both Bush and Chirac were excerpted in the report that followed, and these elite figures defined the meaning of the event in different ways. 'The nations who fought side by side have become partners in peace', Bush said. 'Our alliance for peace is still needed today.' In case the audience at home in Germany had missed the point, the reporter explained that the American president was referring to the situation in Iraq. Chirac was then given considerably more scope to emphasize both that Europeans no longer considered war the proper way to resolve their differences and the importance of European unity rather than Atlantic alliances: 'Nothing could stop a new international order from forming, an order founded on respect for mankind and for the law, on freedom, justice and democracy. [. . .] We hold up the example of Franco-German reconciliation to show the world that hatred has no future, that a path to peace is always possible.' The theme of reconciliation was revisited in a report the following week of another commemoration – that of the 'massacre' of Oradour, when 600 village inhabitants had been 'murdered' by members of an SS unit. For the first time, veterans from Alsace, the part of the country where the unit originated, came to Oradour to pay their respects to the victims.

This, then, was D–Day as depicted by leading broadcasters in countries that had fought each other in two world wars. How was it portrayed in a country that had proclaimed its neutrality throughout both conflicts?

Rapport

That celebrating the past had very much to do with the present, and in particular the current world political situation, was made clear in the Swedish programme as it had been in the German one. The first D–Day story (and there were not many; *Rapport* was the least interested of the six newsrooms in this event) opened with Bush visiting Paris to gain French support for the continued presence of troops in Iraq. After informing viewers that US forces in Baghdad had suffered yet another attack, the report turned to the D–Day anniversary. As in the BBC, veterans were interviewed. They were not British or American, however, but German and Norwegian. One of the Germans, Karl Mass, is interviewed in a cemetery in Normandy. He breaks down in front of the camera, covers his face with his hand, and sobs: 'I weep when I see how many are lying here. [. . .] To this day, I cannot understand' (see plate 5.2).

On 6 June, the Swedish broadcast announced that winners and losers had gathered in Normandy. Like all the others, it led with the commemoration of D–Day which, according to the headlines, 'determined the future of Western Europe'. Again the current affairs frame was in evidence, as the anchor opened the report by saying that the anniversary was turning into a summit between the US, Russia and European leaders.

As the German newsroom had done, *Rapport* stressed the international nature of the gathering, mentioning the presence of twenty-two heads of state and government from sixteen countries,

Plate 5.2   Karl Mass during an interview in a Normandy cemetery

as well as veterans from Norway and Poland, and not just the US and the UK. And, as the German correspondent had done, the Swedish reporter covering the event drew attention to the military and historical enthusiasts play-acting at war. Swedish reporting of the commemoration lacked the solemnity – the almost religious overtones – of the BBC stories. Although Chirac was quoted at some length, it was intimated that the façade of unity was just that: a brave face put on for the crowd, just as the military enthusiasts had put on their period costumes.

On the other hand, the Swedish programme offered viewers something the other two newsrooms mentioned so far did not: the perspective of a woman. As depicted in this news item, Mary Crofton (see plate 5.3) was neither a hero nor a victim. She took an active part in the Normandy invasion, but not as a combatant. She was a nurse, and Swedish viewers were told she had mixed feelings about the enthusiastic re-enactment 'because so many never came back. I mean, many in our generation didn't come back. I mean we were all very young, but when you think half of them weren't going to come back, most of us just feel sad really.' [4]

By this point, it should be evident that there were interesting national differences in D-Day reporting. How do they compare to the coverage of the three newsrooms broadcasting to the global village?

Plate 5.3   Mary Crofton talking about her part in D-Day

BBC World News

In BBC World, as in its sister programme broadcasting to Britons
in a national setting, the rumble of artillery and blasts of exploding
car bombs in Iraq could be heard continually in the background
throughout the sample period. As mentioned in chapter 2, the
World News was populated by political and military leaders, and
the primary definers tended to be men. Several of the D-Day
items broadcast by BBC World to a global audience were virtually the same as those featured on the domestic channel. But most
of them were different – that is, some different topics were dealt
with differently and different reporters were used. The sentiments
expressed were very much the same, however.

BBC World was somewhat more international in its take on
D-Day than its domestic counterpart. Its Paris correspondent
reported on the publication of a book in France that was a com-
pilation of letters and diaries kept by veterans and civilians at the
time of the invasion. By spreading the remarkable stories of those

who lived through D-Day, explained the correspondent, French journalist Jean-Pierre Gueno 'hopes to keep alive these memories for a younger generation in France': 'They will never forget that freedom came from the ocean, thanks to American and British people.'[5] Sixty years on, the reporter continued, the 'momentous' events of that day are still 'seared' into people's minds, and the commemoration provides a chance to honour those who risked and lost their lives to liberate France. The narrative gaze thus switches back to heroes – back from the present glimpsed in the German and Swedish programmes to the past so thoroughly experienced in the domestic British channel. And it remained fixed there up until the commemoration itself.

On 5 June, the reporter on site told the anchor about the day of celebration he had witnessed: 'we've had pageants, we've had pomp and ceremony and spectacle'. He spoke at length about the unflagging old soldiers. Prince Charles had drawn some attention, 'but the real stars today were the veterans themselves, nearly all of them over eighty years old. And what stamina, what fortitude [. . .] they were absolutely unfailing.' It was a theme he returned to repeatedly.

> If you said they were a hero, all of them, *all* of them pooh-poohed that suggestion. In fact one of them, with a military cross I spotted, I said to him, 'That's a fantastic award. You must have done something very great to get that.' He just smiled and said no, they handed it out with the rations.

The day of the most important ceremony, 6 June, was described by one BBC World reporter as 'a day of words and images which have stirred strong memories'. Chirac was quoted here too, talking not of reconciliation and peace, as in the German and Swedish programmes, but of brave men: 'The world is watching us. It sees free people honouring the finest of their heroes. It sees loyal peoples remembering the sacrifices made.' Chancellor Schröder was also quoted as saying that 'they know, and we know, that their death was not in vain'. In the final debriefing at the end of the programme (D-Day both opened and closed the newscast) the anchor asked one of the reporters in Normandy about 'the very strong symbolism' of Schröder speaking at the commemoration. The reporter replied:

> I think the remarkable thing is that it caused so little controversy. There were a few mumblings and grumblings about it, but most vets I've spoken to said they had nothing against the German people [. . .] And there's a certain rapprochement now of course between the German people and the British and the Americans and so on.

The anchor ended the programme in uncharacteristic fashion, by inviting viewers to remember that day, sixty years ago. As he said good night, the BBC World logo merged with the shadowy visages of Allied soldiers, and a succession of black-and-white images passed across the screen to the accompaniment of the BBC World signature theme. It underlined how clearly the news had merged with old battles in the BBC World discourse.

Deutsche Welle

The D-Day anniversary was reported on Deutsche Welle, as it had been in *Heute*, without voices being raised. Chancellor Schröder was somewhat more in focus, but the commemoration was covered as an international affair (DW was the only channel to mention the Canadians as often as the British). Much of the footage was familiar from the other channels. The viewers did not get as close to the participants as people sitting in front of other television screens, but they did get to hear more of the political rhetoric, especially from the two leaders at the heart of European integration. While the Iraq war was rarely mentioned, D-Day was as much about the present, the current state of international relations, as it was about the past.

Like their colleagues in the domestic German and Swedish newsrooms, the Anglo-Saxon journalists at Deutsche Welle drew attention to the disparity between the enthusiasm of people dressing up in period costume to re-enact the invasion and the sombre memories of 'those who lived it'. The retired actor who featured in the BBC is seen in one of the first D-Day reports on this channel, but no reference is made to his lament about continuing bloodshed and war. In Deutsche Welle the juxtaposition of the enthusiastic 'now' and the sombre, remembered 'then' reinforces a recurrent theme: the world of 2004 had become a very different place from that of 1944. Among other things, it was much more cosmopolitan.

The primary definer here is Chancellor Schröder. In a story that documents the arrival in Normandy of veterans from all over the world, mention is made of criticism levelled by the conservative opposition in Germany of Schröder's plans for the commemoration. The conservatives were of the view that the chancellor should pay tribute to the German war dead at the cemetery where most were buried in Normandy. But it was a purely German cemetery, and Schröder had chosen instead to honour fallen soldiers at an international graveyard. 'I am going to visit a war cemetery where eight nations are buried, including 300 German soldiers, as well as Allied troops. I think it is important that we hold common memorial services.' In his speech on 6 June, reproduced at length by Deutsche Welle, Schröder returned to the notion of common fates. He said that Germans knew who had perpetrated the war and were aware of their 'responsibility before history'. Thousands of Allied soldiers paid the highest price for freedom on D-Day, while Germans died because they had been sent on a murderous campaign to colonize Europe. 'But in death', said Schröder, 'all soldiers were united.' The metaphor of mixed marriage was deployed here, in a narrative within a narrative. The reporter said that the chancellor had told the story of a German soldier who had fought in Normandy, been captured and, when released, married a French woman and settled there. The soldier had said that was the beginning of a new happier life. The reporter opined that Schröder had told the story because he too viewed D-Day as an essentially positive date for Germany: it was the date when Germany's own liberation began.

At the end of the day, the Deutsche Welle anchor in Berlin asked the correspondent in Normandy the same question posed throughout this chapter: why was this anniversary so important? The reporter began by giving the same reason as his colleagues on other channels had done, namely that it was probably the last time most of the D-Day veterans would be able to attend. But he then went on to speak of the 'huge significance' of the fact that a German leader had been invited to attend for the first time. It was a demonstration, he said, that the postwar period was now truly over, that Germany had completed its long journey to the West, and that the country 'is now a fully fledged member, a fully respected member of the international community'. The reporter pointed out that most of the veterans with whom he had spoken took no exception to Schröder's presence, that an opinion survey of Normandy inhabitants indicated that 83 per cent of them considered Germany to be their closest ally and thought 'it's time to draw a line under the past'. But, said the reporter in the final debriefing, there was something else happening in the background:

> . . . and that is, well, I was talking to a couple of French colleagues and they told me that, compared with the fiftieth anniversary, this anniversary carried much more emotion. Part of that seems to have to do with the fact that Chancellor Schröder was here. It seems that, for the French especially, it's reassuring to see the leader of the country that was once their mortal enemy is now such a good friend that you can come and join them at this kind of commemoration.

So while the global German broadcaster acknowledged the emotional content of the event, just as its British colleague and the channel targeting a domestic British audience had done, it was interpreted in quite a different way. Here, people were moved not (just) at the thought of comrades who had fallen six decades before, but at the thought of how former enemies had overcome their differences and become such good friends. As depicted on Deutsche Welle, the D-Day anniversary showed 'just how much the world has changed in the last six decades'.

EuroNews

Two themes were dominant in EuroNews coverage of the D-Day anniversary and events leading up to and following it. One was the cost of war, then and now. The other was the importance of overcoming past differences and celebrating new partnerships. As could be expected, the D-Day events as depicted in EuroNews had a more international flavour than in the accounts of the domestic broadcasters in general, and the BBC in particular.

In a report of the sixtieth anniversary of the Battle of Montecassino, for example, viewers were told that Polish troops cleared the way for the British and American advance on Rome by taking Montecassino monastery. 'But victory came at a heavy cost. Many historians refer to the Battle of Montecassino as the Stalingrad of the West because of its large number of casualties.'[6] A week later, covering the tribute paid to the soldiers who died in the 1944 Anzio campaign, a US veteran talked about what the liberation of Rome entailed. Like the men seen in other broadcasts, he was conquered by his emotions: 'The cost was very high. In those four months, the total casualties amounted to 28,000, killed, missing, wounded – 28,000 [*breaks down*]. And here, many of our comrades . . . [*can't speak, shakes head*]. They rest in peace now.'

Not only did EuroNews viewers learn that Poles had been among those to drive the Nazis out of Europe; they were also informed that the French were actors as well as victims. In a report in the section of the news half-hour called *Europeans* (introduced, as ever, with the words 'The questions and challenges facing us all now . . .'), a veteran called Léon Gautier gave his account of the landing in which he took part. As in the other channels, his narrative is aided by black-and-white footage and music from the period. And, as they were in the other EuroNews reports, viewers are reminded that Léon and his contemporaries 'paid a huge price in terms of human lives'. The report contains several narratives, all of which share a cosmopolitan frame. Apart from Léon, who joined soldiers in another country to fight for freedom and democracy, the report features an interview with two D-Day survivors – an American and a German who was in the Wehrmacht – both of whom married French women and moved to France. In his narrative (within the larger narrative), the American, Bill Coleman, tells of his experiences landing at Omaha Beach and explains why he decided to move with his wife to France. The resolution of his narrative fits into the overarching EuroNews theme of reconciliation. The Bill that speaks about the right of Germans to mourn their dead on the anniversary of D–Day is familiar from Hannerz's definition of a cosmopolitan as someone who can deal with diversity in human thought, experience and ways of life: 'You're honouring those who died. And that's any and every cemetery here. That people died for the cause they thought was right regardless of what side they were on.'

The narrative of the German, Hans Flindt, and his French wife, Marie-Thérèse (who may or may not be the couple referred to by Chancellor Schröder in Deutsche Welle), picks up where Bill's resolves. Here, the purpose of remembering is dealt with more explicitly. Far away from the costumes and re-enactment and old military vehicles converging on the Normandy beaches, this EuroNews report takes the viewer to an idyllic white cottage in the French countryside and a green garden alive with birdsong. The camera shows Hans and Marie-Thérèse working contentedly side by side. Hans is dressed like an archetypical French peasant, in smock and beret. The voiceover explains that he was nineteen years old when taken prisoner in 1944, was freed three years later, and met his wife while working on a farm. Then a macro-dimension is placed on top of the microcosm: the presence of Chancellor Schröder at the commemoration is mentioned, and the fact that there has been little objection to his presence. But Schröder is not the only one to receive an invitation for the first time, it turns out. Marie-Thérèse talks about the significance of the Flindts having been asked to take part in a symposium on peace the previous month. She says that, until the symposium, her husband had refused to talk about the war and his experiences of it. 'The first stories I heard from Hans, I heard them at the war memorial', she says. 'When we married, all we wanted was that everyone got along.' In explaining his reticence, Hans returns to the theme of the cost of war.

The camera cuts at this point to a shot of children running through a military cemetery (see plate 5.4), and the larger EuroNews narrative shifts from the costs of an old war to those of a conflict in the present. The reporter tells us, 'There's an underlying feeling that, while D–Day was a just and noble cause, today thousands of Americans are fighting a war that has little international support.' Confirmation for this is sought from a French writer:

Plate 5.4   The fallen support a new generation

This will be a very special anniversary of the landings, precisely because we are going to celebrate, if one can put it like that, the arrival in 1944 of 'America the Good' at the very moment that a useless and atrocious war is being waged in Iraq by 'America the Bad'. To say that the US army in Iraq has a rapport with the American soldiers of 1944 is in a way to dishonour the people of '44.[7]

So far, the only other broadcaster to give a speaking part to a woman in a D-Day narrative was Swedish television. Two days after EuroNews put a microphone in front of Marie-Thérèse Flindt, another report highlighted the experiences of women and non-combatants at the time of Normandy heroism. In a story broadcast on 3 June, EuroNews took viewers to occupied Paris where, we are told, some formed resistance cells, some grudgingly learned to live with their new masters, and others collaborated in more ways than one. Black-and-white newsreel footage of women having their heads shaved in public (see plate 5.5), to the unkind laughter of the people in the crowds that had gathered to watch, tells a strikingly different story from the happy tale of Marie-Thérèse and Hans.

Alain, the 'fruit' of one such 'forbidden love story', personifies

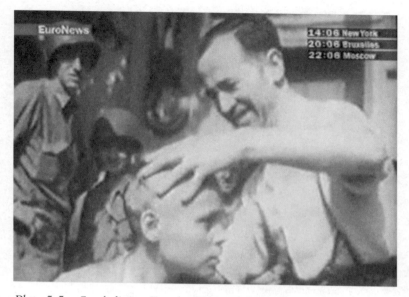

Plate 5.5   Symbolizing French–German relations in wartime

the many war children who were forced to live in secret or shame. He talks about being bullied as a child and of his search to find out about his father. This is implied to be an important part of the work involved in understanding who you are – coming to terms with the past by trying to find out about it. Like Hans Flindt, who had refused to speak of the war until invited to the peace symposium, many of the mothers of the 'little Krauts' remained silent on the subject of their children's German fathers. Alain has chosen not to accept this. The bad news is that he is unlikely to succeed: looking for a Lieutenant Schulz in the German archives is like trying to find a John Smith in England. The good news (the resolution of the narrative) returns us to the EuroNews theme of reconciliation: 'Thankfully', says the reporter at the end of the story, 'these people are no longer pariahs in society.'

    The anniversary of D-Day itself was paid considerable attention in EuroNews as it had been in the other channels. Viewers were provided with a vista on the Normandy beaches of military fans and amateur historians dressed up in uniforms for the occasion, and offered a history lesson illustrated with the by now ubiquitous

Plate 5.6   Symbolizing French–German relations in peacetime

newsreel footage. World leaders spoke eloquently and at length
at the commemoration, as can be seen from the transcripts of the
complete speeches of Chirac, Bush and Schröder available on
official government websites. Given that none of these speeches
were reproduced in their entirety on any of the channels reviewed
here, it is interesting to see which of the speakers were given most
airtime and what parts of the speeches were excerpted. In EuroNews,
Schröder and Chirac were the central figures, and the trajectory
taken 'from enemies to allies' was emphasized in the headlines, in
the choreography of embraces on which the camera lingered, and
in the parts of the speeches that were relayed to EuroNews viewers.
'The military cemeteries and the scars of the two world wars have
left the people of Europe, and especially the German people, with
a permanent duty, resisting racism, anti-Semitism and totalitarian
ideologies', said Schröder. But it was Chirac who could, following
Stuart Hall (1994), be called the 'primary definer': 'We express our
common will to continue together on the path of Europe, united
around its values, reconciled with itself, with its geography, with
its history and culture' (see plate 5.6).[8]

Across the skies depicted on EuroNews, the same aircraft flew in the same formation, trailing the same colours as on the other television screens. But the flyover here was not said to be a tribute to the victorious liberation army. It was 'a tribute to those who resisted the Nazis, including those inside Germany itself'. In the discourse of EuroNews, Europe had apparently found the strength referred to by Arendt, to put that which is too close at a certain distance, where it can be seen and understood.

Lessons learned

The man quoted at the beginning of this chapter as telling a reporter that people had forgotten about the Second World War was interviewed in a bar. This may explain his remark. Had he instead been at home, in front of his television, with the news switched on, his view might have been different. Granted, no US news programmes have been analysed here but, given the leading role played by President Bush and the American veterans, it is unlikely that any of the networks would have ignored the D-Day commemoration. No speculation is needed when it comes to the six European broadcasters dealt with in this chapter. The results show that neither the newsrooms nor the political actors to whom they gave airtime had forgotten the war. More to the point, they apparently wanted to make sure that their audiences remembered it and reflected on its meaning.

The question guiding these past few pages took its cue from the man in the bar. His claim was operationalized by asking: What *did* these broadcasters say that people did in the war? Who were those people? And what do these stories seem to be telling us about how people solve problems that transcend national borders?

The story told by the national British channel – its master narrative if you will – was that heroes liberated the oppressed during the war. In his speeches, President Bush tried to equate the liberation of Europe with the liberation of Iraq. The BBC resisted this frame to some extent. In the days surrounding the commemoration, the fallout from the Iraq invasion and the task of selling a handover plan to the UN was an American mission, fraught with problems. The D-Day invasion, on the other hand – a drama starring British soldiers with an international supporting cast – was a glorious success and an uncontestedly good cause. The heroes in question are unusual figures in BBC discourse, which other studies have shown tends to privilege elites. Here the focus was on the ordinary men, often with working-class and regional dialects, who were repeatedly celebrated as belonging to the most noble and self-effacing of generations. The story told to BBC viewers was about the experiences of these men. It was about something that happened six decades ago, and had little to say about the current state of international relations apart from the fact that viewers had them to thank for freedom.

The story told by *Heute* to domestic German audiences, on the other hand, was about the present. D-Day had to do with the birth of modern Germany and the importance of having friends, and keeping them. The people in this story were Europeans who had overcome their differences and learned to respect each other. While war veterans featured in this narrative, the main actors were Schröder and Chirac, or the Germany and France they symbolize.

The Swedish answer to the question of what people did in the war – especially when seen against the background of SVT coverage of international affairs in general – seems to be: 'wasting valuable lives'. In contrast to the profoundly gendered and militaristic BBC discourse, the Swedish newsroom offered viewers the perspective of a woman and a non-combatant. Instead of revelling in the enthusiasm of the military replay, the nurse gave voice to all those who lived through the carnage, missed those who did not survive, and just felt sad. Also in contrast to its British counterpart, the Swedish newsroom understood the D-Day anniversary to be only ostensibly about the past. What made it interesting was that it provided an occasion for world leaders to have a summit and sort out their differences over Iraq.

Rather than painting a different picture from the newsrooms servicing domestic audiences, the global channels tended to reinforce national tendencies, at least in the cases where there was a domestic sibling. As could be expected, they focused somewhat less on the nations in which they were based than their domestic counterparts and opened their windows on a wider world. In the case of BBC World, this involved the inclusion of a report on French memories and the mention of German and Russian participants. But both story and discourse were strongly reminiscent of the domestic British newsroom, with their 'Boy's Own' tone of coverage and the situating of the D-Day story – and by corollary those listening to it – firmly in the past. The BBC World narrative of the Normandy invasion was a closed text of liberation and heroism. By contrast, the global German newsroom told the story in a respectful rather than a worshipful tone of voice. This narrative was not one of American and British liberators who had long ago fought shoulder to shoulder for a just cause, but one of Europeans who were living in the present as the best of friends. The metaphor employed was actually stronger: the D-Day anniversary provided the opportunity to reaffirm the marriage vows between a partner who had once been raped and her violator, who had regretted his evil ways and become trustworthy and steadfast.

But, of all the channels, it was EuroNews that made most of the theme of reconciliation. What did people do in the war? Behave badly, was the answer given by EuroNews – both now, in Iraq, and then, in Auschwitz, Oradour and Paris, when women who had fallen in love with men from the wrong country were made into pariahs. EuroNews acknowledged, like the others, that many had behaved in a human and altruistic fashion. Who were these people? As in the BBC discourse, they were American and British soldiers. But in the EuroNews account of the liberation of Europe from barbarity they also came from the new EU member states. EuroNews did more than echo the Deutsche Welle metaphor of mixed marriage. It amplified it. On EuroNews, the sixtieth anniversary of D-Day was celebrated by a Europe that was reconciled with itself. What it said about contemporary international relations was that the world had moved on and was no longer a place in which differences could be resolved by military conflict. Where both BBC programmes had symbolized D-Day in logos featuring a gun, in EuroNews it was epitomized by the passionate embrace of the French and German leaders.

Lest we forget

Reams have been devoted in recent decades to the impact of the media on spatial relations. It has become a commonplace to say that the technological changes embodied in the metaphor of the 24/7 newsroom have 'shrunk the planet' and given us a berth in McLuhan's global village (Robertson 1999). Considerably less work has been done on the media's impact on the temporal dimensions of social life and political consciousness (Stevenson 1995: 114). It is perhaps for this reason that a dominant theme in the debate about media power has to do with the myopia induced by the 'breaking news' syndrome. The complaint has been made by many that, before the audience has a chance to make sense of what is happening, today's news is replaced by newer news. Few have put it more eloquently than the journalist who complained that 'Changing reflections threaten the citizen's most elementary weapon of self-defence: memory. As episodes are presented, then dexterously whipped away and replaced with others, the sense of continuity is lost' (Ascherson 1988: 86). Long before Ascherson – as long ago as 1941 – Lazarsfeld complained that 'continually new news programmes keep us from ever finding out the details of the previous news'.

The results of this brief detour into the realm of mediated historicity indicate that such claims are problematic. They overlook the narrative power of reports such as those considered in this chapter; they assume that news is all 'data' and no 'theory', to borrow the terminology of Peffley and Hurwitz. Even if the BBC reporters in particular left few blanks for viewers to fill in, the etcetera law was at work in all of the D-Day reports. It was a matter of brushing up on knowledge that is, as Featherstone has put it, 'relatively fixed; that is, it has persisted over time and may incorporate rituals, symbols and ceremonies that link people to a place and a common sense of the past.' It is a sense of belonging, of home 'sustained by collective memory' (Featherstone 1995: 92–4). Television news can and often does serve as the site for rehearsing familiar themes, nourishing shared understandings, and fanning the embers of collective memories. The challenge for the scholar is to establish the contexts in which the embers are blown into flames and dormant memories become active. It is not the technology of communication that is the issue here, but how it used. If, as the journalist quoted above maintains, continuity is lost, then it is not necessarily because episodes are whipped away. It could be because they are deployed in new contexts, where they take on different meanings.

So what *does* it mean when old wars turn up in the news? At its most basic, it means that someone is trying to tell the viewer how 'we' (be it Britons, Germans, Swedes, Europeans or citizens of the free world) got from there to here (be it the beginning of a new chapter or the end of history). In some of the news discourses examined here, D–Day (and Reagan and EU enlargement) reports illustrate what Thompson referred to as the legitimation aspect of tradition, and were in this respect ideological. In the two BBC programmes, the recurrence of Bush and the scope given to his rhetoric about the need to come to the aid of those oppressed by undemocratic regimes, and the recurrence of the word 'liberation', are messages to publics with a stake in the Iraq war. By contrast, the emphasis placed by the Swedish and German broadcasters and by EuroNews on the human cost of warfare and the importance of reconciliation and partnership speaks the language of EU politics. An identity aspect is also easily discerned in the reports of all the six channels, when viewers are clearly addressed as 'part of a social group which has a history of its own and a collective fate'. The difference is that, in some of these stories, the social group has evolved. The 'we' who is being depicted and at the same time addressed has in many of these items become European, and the collective that now shares a fate is comprised of both good guys and former bad guys. As Thompson (1995: 194) explains, the identity-forming aspect of tradition has not been eliminated, it has only been reshaped, and, in this, media actors have a responsibility.

The pace of technological development has not abated in the interval between the broadcasting of the news programmes revisited here and the writing of this book. Quite the opposite. Bulletins produced by these newsrooms can now be viewed on mobile phone or as a podcast, and press journalists are competing with their television colleagues by broadcasting on the websites of

Plate 5.7   EuroNews urges viewers to remember historical atrocities and reflect on how reconciliation has become possible

their newspapers. This need not mean that the storytelling function of television news has become less important, however. As the busy inhabitants of the global village turn increasingly to the internet to skim the facts of breaking news, television news broadcasts have been given more scope to go in-depth, even to develop a more documentary style of reporting.

'They have the power reserved for places where history was fashioned', a BBC reporter solemnly declared on 4 June 2004, speaking of the Normandy beaches being panned to his voice-over. Two days later on EuroNews, the coda was provided not by words, but by an image. An item on another Second World War commemoration ended with a lingering close-up of the sign at the gates of the village of Oradour, once the site of a massacre and now (in the EuroNews narrative) the site of reconciliation between French and Germans (see plate 5.7).[9] The sign admonished Europeans of today to remember. The argument of this chapter has been that the journalist could just as well have been referring to the discursive construction sites constituted by his reports, and those of colleagues in other newsrooms, both then and now. The lesson learned, this time not of history but of the work of imagination underlying cosmopolitanization, is that the development of a sense of humanity as a whole, and of a transcending sense of civic and humanitarian responsibility, has more than a spatial dimension. It has a temporal one as well.

6

Brushing away the Flies: Concluding Thoughts

'When we see starving children with flies on their faces, we distance ourselves', to quote a foreign correspondent who featured in chapter 3 of this book. 'When we see a Swede brush the flies away we notice, we say, "Oh, look, there are flies".' He was trying to explain the challenges involved in reporting complicated events taking place in a complicated world to faraway audiences with lives that were also complicated (albeit in different ways), and whose attentiveness could not be taken for granted. It is, of course, not a specifically Swedish experience. Pictures of suffering children with flies on their faces are a central feature of journalistic iconography, and were deployed in all the newsrooms studied here – for example in German coverage of the Dafur crisis (see plate 6.1).

In a globalizing world, the assumption can no longer be that media behaviour in the settings of national democracy is what really counts. More than ever, media power has to do with how people understand the world and their place in it, and it may thus matter whose hand (if any) is brushing away the flies. At stake here is more than whether viewers are told about starving children. It could also matter whether they are told that the world is characterized by cooperation or conflict, whether its problems are something that should concern them, and whether they are

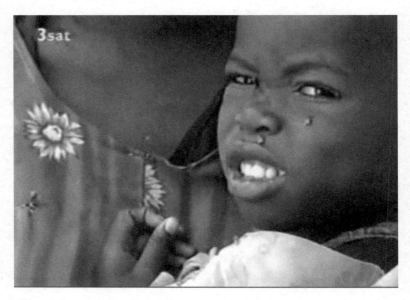

Plate 6.1   A starving child with flies on her face[1]

portrayed as having obligations to, or at least things in common
with, people beyond the borders of their own nation. As those
depictions vary, so might the preconditions for the cosmopolitan
education advocated by Nussbaum. News, as Seaton (2003: 47)
says, is 'how we know ourselves and the world'. This book has
asked whether different publics are told different stories about the
world, and may thus come to know it in different ways.

Getting here from there

The debate between the 'optimists' and the 'pessimists' has tended
to focus on the virtues and vices of media actors and technology
in an absolute sense. Less attention has been paid to the uses to
which that technology is actually put. The words of the journalist
who speaks about brushing away flies indicate that professionals
(like him) proffer viewers (like us) images to which we are meant
to respond. They also indicate that responses are more likely to

be forthcoming if something is added to the image that brings it into focus – something that serves to nourish the imagination of the spectator. The journalist also speaks in a way that resonates with Boltanski's (1999) understanding of the work involved. As explained earlier, his account of spectatorship has two levels. The first is that of the witness who views suffering directly, and who acts by relaying news of it to absent others. The second is the level of such absentees, whose experience is mediated rather than direct. By referring to what 'we' see, the journalist positions himself both as the first-level spectator who must impart something of importance to a distant viewer, presumably in such a way as to reduce the distance, at least in experiential terms, *and* as the second-level spectator who has himself consumed many media products and is well aware of his own reasons for often failing to respond. Whether situated on the first or the second level, imaginative work is required of these actors.

While primarily an empirical contribution to a largely theoretical debate, this book has nevertheless had normative underpinnings. Chief among these is the conviction that the power of the news media in a globalized world extends beyond the imparting of accurate, impartial and reliable information so esteemed by opinion leaders and many of the public service broadcasters whose output has been analysed in the preceding pages. The power of the news media in general, and television in particular, also resides in its potential to engage its viewers, as well as to inform them; to help them remember as well as to know; and to make it possible for them to recognize and identify with the distant Others who populate their television screens, rather than just to sit back and play the role of spectator. Nevertheless, the ideas expressed here have grown out of analyses of how accounts of the world, and messages about the relationship of the intended audience to that world, are actually deployed in different news cultures. Its overarching 'optimism' is tempered by empirical insights which suggest that the consciousness–raising potential of television is operationalized differently in different cultures. From a methodological perspective, it has been argued that, in order to gain purchase on these differences and to explicate the different dimensions of power involved, it is necessary to use a combination of analytical instruments, both quantitative and interpretive. By attending to the narrative techniques employed in 'reporting the world back to itself', it is possible to explore the sort of media power that Stevenson, writing of cosmopolitanism, has referred to as 'the capacity to throw into question established codes and to rework frameworks of understanding' (Stevenson 2003: 4).

The focus of this book, then, has been on television news narratives and their potential power to engage rather than inform – their potential to cultivate cosmopolitan outlooks by sophistication. It has been suggested that this power can be performed in different ways, to different degrees or on different dimensions. The first has to do with the promotion of *awareness*. What is happening in the world, and where? To whom is it happening? Here, perhaps, is the locus of what Beck refers to as 'latent cosmopolitanism'. The second involves the activation of that which concerns Boltanski and Chouliaraki – the appeal to pity, or at least sympathy. But the people I feel sorry for may not necessarily be like me; they may not belong in my world. It has been argued that a distinction should be made between engagement in this dimension and a third sort, which is possible in a Meyrowitzian 'placeless' world. When news narratives invite identification, the viewer is encouraged to imagine that the distant other is not distant at all.

Like that of Nava, the argument pursued in this book emerged from a study of specific narratives, and, like hers, it differs from much social science work on cosmopolitanism, which is 'largely conceptual' in origin (Nava 2007: 5). Another similarity is that the focus has been not on elites, but on the sort of 'ordinary' people at whom the semiotic materials circulating in public discourse are directed. An important question is thus how the average viewer makes sense of the sort of news stories with which this book is concerned – if in fact he or she takes notice of them at all. Focus group interviews convened in the same weeks as the news stories were broadcast, reported in chapter 3, sought an answer to that question. The interviews were intended to generate insights both into how people make sense of the outside world and into how the media might contribute to that sense-making. In other words, they explored the role television news reports could be thought to play in developing mental 'maps' (Hall 1994: 207; Ruddock

2001). Analysis of their 'talk' showed that, while some respondents thought they had 'turned off', unable to deal with all the misery and terror contained in news reports and fearful of becoming 'numbed' (an operationalization, in the vernacular, of Moeller's notion of 'compassion fatigue'), they had in fact internalized the narrative structures of the television news stories made for people like them.

Routine news reporting, it has been seen, does not just give cues about distance and proximity in a geographical sense, through virtual spatial experiences. The television news texts that were fished up in the weeks trawled here were replete with stories about belonging to historical communities and the ritual celebration of temporal experiences. The death and funeral of ex-president Ronald Reagan (followed in considerable detail by the two British broadcasters but covered by the other four channels as well) occasioned a prolonged flashback to the Cold War. It was a theme that had already been activated by the accession to the EU of former Warsaw Pact states. In the EU enlargement narratives, the focus was on the end of the Cold War; in the Reagan stories it was on its zenith. In both cases, it was as though a question was being posed to some unspecified collective: 'How did we get here from there?' Historical imaginations were activated by earlier wars as well. For the Germans, EU enlargement involved crossing many bridges between cities and countries that had been divided by the Second World War. The sixtieth anniversary of D-Day provided all six newsrooms with material for narratives on the importance of international cooperation to protect democracy and secure for coming generations a world in which human rights and dignity were respected. Such news discourse has, perhaps surprisingly, a good deal to say to the study of cosmopolitanism, despite the scepticism of authors such as Smith. He argues that the 'images and symbols that have obtained a hold on human imagination' are historically specific and spatially limited (Smith 1990: 178). Be that as it may, the D-Day narratives show that it need not be only in national settings that they can be revived and reworked. Parallel to the nationalist frames of BBC coverage was a cosmopolitan discourse that used the same event and images (although sometimes other symbolism) to tell a different story. There are thus empirical as well as theoretical reasons for defending the view, discussed in chapter 5, that the media, as one of the main mnemonic sites in contemporary society, could be contributing to a sense of belonging to a larger collectivity by forging imagined social relationships that extend across time as well as space. This is a possibility foreshadowed by Boulding's remark of 1959, which opened chapter 1, that images of the collectivity extend from a recorded or mythological past and into an imagined future. While he and Smith were preoccupied with the nation, our thinking need not stay there. As Holton has concluded, cosmopolitanism is tied up with particular histories, memories and places (like the beaches of Normandy), which means that cosmopolitanism is situated in time as well as space. The conclusion of this book is the same as his – that there are many cosmopolitanisms, 'rather than a singular unitary freefloating cosmopolitanism that transcends context and relations with particulars' (Holton 2009: 193).

As well as the broader issue of whether cosmopolitanism is best understood as a form of universalism or, as here, as contextualized and respectful of difference, there is an immediate issue related to research design. This has to do with how far the results of this study can be generalized. The material which generated them is large – perhaps unusually so. But the worlds that have been explored have been seen through Northern European eyes, or camera lenses. Even the global broadcasters featured in this book work in reasonably specific, timebound settings (which is why, after all, it is possible to challenge the pessimism of someone like Smith). How particular are the insights gleaned from the results of this study? It could be argued that the most significant finding is how different the world can look, even when observed from geographically and culturally proximate vantage points. It thus seems likely that the conclusions would only be strengthened by the incorporation of newsrooms from Asia, Latin America or Africa, with vantage points that are geographically distant from those studied here, and which may have different cultural and historical references on which to draw. One task for further research is to widen the scope of such comparison; another is to explore how the world looks when the discursive gaze is reversed and Europe is the 'other', for example in counter-hegemonic media such as Al Jazeera.

Telling the difference

Narratives take particular events as their reference point, news handle or point of departure. The observation made by Bruner (1991: 6) that this is their vehicle rather than their destination resonates with the newsroom stories analysed here. Just as a family car can be steered by different drivers and used to travel in different directions, so can narratives convey readers and viewers to different, and perhaps unexpected, destinations.

The sort of results presented in figure 2.1 (p. 39; the diagram in which BBC World scores so highly) can be misleading if the objective is to understand if and how television news could work on the cosmopolitanism that Beck maintains is latent in many more people than is generally thought, and transform it into a more active variety. If people feel at home where it is safe, and not at home where there is conflict (as the focus group discussions indicated), then it is worth noting that the world portrayed in some (German, Swedish and 'European') newsrooms tends to be characterized by cooperation, and not just the conflict that is omnipresent in other (British) newsrooms.

The news media are often accused of 'dumbing down' and proffering superficial accounts of the world. But, as argued by Cottle and Rai (2008), we must be sensitive to the complexity inherent in many news reports. If nothing else, this book provides a cautionary tale, warning against generalizations about the way the media work and the homogeneity of accounts of the world propounded in the global newsroom.

Seen in all their banality, as daily doses of the medicine prescribed to the well-informed citizen (the cosmopolitan of the civic variety), the news reports featured here have a good deal in common. When it comes to 'news coverage for special occasions', such as devastating floods, the rewriting of the map of Europe, the live reporting of old battles or the death of Cold Warriors, the values manifested in the choice of, and attention given to, news events also show many common features. But when one looks beyond *what* is being told and pays attention to *how* it is being related – when one attends to discourse as well as story – then the evidence presented here suggests that cosmopolitanism on a cultural level has different preconditions.

Of the six newsrooms studied here, it is the British (both national and global in their remit), on the one hand, and the Swedish, on the other, that represent the opposite ends of the spectrum.

Swedish accounts of the world tend to be about the human consequences of the actions of governments, bureaucracies and political leaders – actions that do not always make sense. They are in keeping with a theme that recurs in SVT news stories over time (see Robertson 2000). Conflict and human suffering are not inevitable but often the result of officialdom. If only they are allowed to get on with their industrious lives, ordinary people tend to live harmoniously: this is the 'myth' (in the Barthian sense) or master narrative of the Swedish newsroom.

By way of contrast, what seems to be taken for granted – that which 'goes without saying' in the BBC context – is that there is something inevitable about the suffering we see when we open a window on the world. The worldview refracted here is 'realist' both in the sense of literary convention and in the way it is used in international relations theory: there will always be wars, there will always be refugees, there will always be suffering; the commentators do no let foul play go past unnoticed, but ultimately not much can be done – certainly not by 'you' (the viewer on the couch), a spectator of events at a distance. But there is also an undertone of reassurance: there are capable elites out there taking care of troubling events, which tend to happen to 'others'. While the realist techniques of the omniscient BBC World narrator (and, to a lesser extent, the BBC *10 O'Clock News* pedagogue) keep us in the place of the innocent bystander (or wide-eyed listener at the fireside as the mud-stained foreign correspondent recounts what he – or more often she – has heard on his or her travels), the naturalist devices deployed by the Swedish narrators (who take us into the kitchen of an Indian schoolteacher or walk us beside a family leaving the Warsaw Pact to join their friends in Europe) more often seem to be telling the audience to imagine what it would be like to be in this person's shoes. The master narrative at work here is that the oppressed can always fight back and that meaningful battles can be waged, if not by the pen against the sword, then by talking and reasoning rather than fighting, by people with whom the viewer can identify. Where one newsroom reassures the viewer that competent elites are dealing with these difficult, and inevitable, problems, another newsroom reminds us that we could be the woman with the Samsonite suitcase.

These are telling differences, ingrained in the daily reporting of everyday events, that can easily go unnoticed, given that the story-telling techniques are not always opaque. Silverstone opens his work on *Media and Morality* by reflecting on a BBC radio broadcast with an Afghan blacksmith, who thinks his village is being bombed because Al Qaeda has killed many Americans and their donkeys and destroyed their castles. Silverstone claims that the appearance of the blacksmith, and his version of the world, is relatively rare. For British viewers, claims Silverstone, the Afghan 'is who he is' only on Western screens. 'He has no existence otherwise,' argues Silverstone. 'He, in his unfamiliarity and distance as a speaker, on the one hand, but in his familiarity and closeness as visible or audible presence, on the other, is a presence that those who hear him can neither touch nor interrogate' (Silverstone 2007: 3). While not denying the tactile element, the point of this book has been to problematize this (undeniably compelling) claim. It has been argued that it is, at least partly, an empirical question whether or not the presence of such a figure as the Afghan can be inter-rogated, and that naturalist techniques may, in a way, do just this. Some narratives may invite us to engage in (imagined) dialogue with distant others, even if many may not.

As well as the narratives of the journalists analysed here (con-sisting in their turn of stories told by the people in their reports), this book has conveyed the narrative of a researcher.[2] 'We see what we want to see', a BBC camerawoman once said, describing how she went about shooting a story. 'We film what we know.'[3] We write what we know too, even if the ambition of this author has been to allow herself to be surprised, and to find answers she did not know when she posed the questions guiding the study reported here.

The world of television news

To close the book, a new discussion will be started – or an ongoing conversation rejoined – about norms and news values in a globalizing world, and about cosmopolitan commitments to the people in that world.

As discussed in chapter 2, governing authorities have set out clear guidelines for public service broadcasters operating in a national setting. National news organizations have been given the mission of counteracting prejudice and stereotypical thinking, and of increasing people's awareness and understanding of others who are different from them. The question is what such a responsibility entails when the society extends beyond the borders of the nation. Is it a cosmopolitan responsibility and, if so, what version of cosmopolitanism is suitable? What can and should be expected of news media in a global context?

One of the viewers who featured in chapter 3 expressed sentiments that are probably familiar to many readers. She apparently considered herself to have obligations of what, in the terminology of this study, could be called the political or 'civic' variety of cosmopolitanism. These were obligations to keep abreast of current affairs, to be aware of what was happening in the world. She expressed feelings of inadequacy to do so, and said she felt guilty about not being able to take on board reports of 'war and so on'. The problem she experienced was of not being as moved by seeing lots of people dying as by a single story, with one person telling it. 'It's easier to put yourself in the tragedy then', she said, ashamed. Her lament echoes that of scholars and others who have commented on media performance and identified a problem in 'tabloidization', the 'feminization' of news reporting and 'personification' techniques – in the tendency, under conditions of media globalization, for processes and policies to be under-reported while the gaze is directed at the individual, and increasingly at the 'ordinary person', at the expense of the powerful elites thought to be the ones who change the world. The respondent was speaking of her behaviour during the weeks following 9/11, but her discomfort will be familiar to those who later watched and thought about

Neda, the icon of the 2009 protests in Iran, shot down before their eyes, her death replayed infinitely on broadcast news and YouTube.

The argument pursued here – and which the book gives the opportunity of pursuing beyond it – is that the sort of inadequacy lamented by such voices needs to be reconsidered: not rejected, but looked at from a different angle.

Mediated cosmopolitanism?

The whole world (or significant parts of it) may have watched when Obama was sworn in as US president, but sceptics are right in pointing out that it is not *being* watched on a routine basis. If news reporting is superficial, however, then a thin rendition of the world can be a matter of scope. Many countries, conflicts and collaborative efforts are missed by the searchlight of the television crews. Nevertheless, what *is* caught in the glare of the lights is not always superficial. As Cottle and Rai have observed, reportage is not just the domain of the documentary. This study, it is hoped, has shown that there are repetitive narrative practices which give us cause to question the platitude that television news assaults us with a barrage of perpetually new, disjointed information that we, as viewers, have no chance to make sense of. The sorts of texts explored in earlier chapters are rich veins to mine if we want to understand how members of particular societies may be more readily able to accept some 'realities' than others, and be more open than others to cosmopolitan views of the globalizing world in which we live. The people we may identify with, and our ability to deal with the differences between them and us and feel obligations towards them, may well vary according to the news stories we are told and, most of all, by the way they are told.

After two decades of technological revolution, people have abundant opportunities to become informed about what is happening in their world: the explosion first of commercial broadcasting, and later of internet resources ranging from the websites and podcasts of traditional news organizations to social media such as

Twitter, means that Europeans are no longer reliant on their public service broadcasters if they choose to be well-informed citizens and 'watch the world', as Flickr invites its users to do. This does not mean that television news has lost its importance – or power. On the contrary: in such a setting, television can play a more profound role, and help viewers engage with the world as well as observe it. Parallel to a 'thinning' out of political reporting and the abbreviated communication of the social media, there is evidence to suggest a 'thickening' of reportage culture.

The concern of this book has been to move beyond conjecture and visions of 'frameworlds' and to take a look at what is actually happening in news reporting. Rather than providing clear answers, the results beg new questions, of the sort that Silverstone was so good at posing. Chief among these is what we expect of the media in a multi-outlet, globalizing setting, whatever our views on the virtues of Nussbaum's cosmopolitan education. Do we want television to offer reporters who return, mud-stained and battle-weary, to recount the exciting things they have seen and heard to those of us who have stayed at home? Or do we want correspondents who will take us with them on their adventures, to experience things in close-up, and engage in vicarious dialogue with people who have left the Warsaw Pact to help build a brave new Europe, who are trying to survive in a Sudan blighted by civil war and famine, who are trying to retain their dignity after imprisonment in Abu Ghraib, and who are trying to make a better life in the burgeoning economies of China and India? Our 'understanding of persons from different ethnic and cultural backgrounds', as the policy document referred to in chapter 2 put it, and our awareness of one another, are perhaps best nourished with a diet of stories told by the second sort of reporter. Such workers of the imagination have the capacity to bring us to the Other, or bring the Other to us, or otherwise urge us to consider that 'this could be *me*'. It is in such work that what Beck identifies as a constitutive principle of cosmopolitanism comes into play: that of 'perspective-taking' – the capacity and willingness to put oneself in the position of the other. As Silverstone reminds us, the media provide our symbolic connection to the distant other. They provide a 'thick' moral space in which otherness and sameness are made available to the construction of global imaginaries – 'a sense of there being an elsewhere; a sense of that elsewhere being in some way relevant to me; a sense of my being there' (Silverstone 2007: 10).

In thinking about counterpoint, Silverstone drew attention to the things that the reader of a novel has in common with the viewer of a television news programme. It is an idea well represented by the novelist Steven Galloway (2008: 201–3) in the internal dialogue of a man, Dragan, trying to survive in a besieged Sarajevo. When Dragan looks over a barricade to see a foreign journalist setting up his camera, he decides to move the body of a man killed by snipers while queuing with him for water. It is not that Dragan wants to hide evidence of the atrocity from the world. What bothers him is the thought that the television camera will capture a corpse – a dead body that will not bother anyone – rather than the person who used to inhabit it. Viewers of the evening news all over the world 'may remark on the horror, but they will, most likely, think nothing of it at all'. Brushing away the flies, Dragan looks at the corpse and reflects that he knows nothing about the man it used to be. 'But that doesn't matter. This man is him. Or could be.' The character in Galloway's novel, the librarian who feels badly for thinking of the fate of an individual rather than the thousands who are dying around the world, and the journalist who saw herself in the woman with the Samsonite suitcase were all capturing the dialectic of mediated cosmopolitanism, which is at once inevitable and an impossibility.

Notes

Preface

1 At least, that is the impression given by the title of the directive that was for many years the lynchpin of EU communication policy. In fact, *Television Without Frontiers* contained a substantial dose of economic and cultural protectionism.

2 The problem of defining news, or rather distinguishing journalism from other information, is an even trickier question, which must be left to another study.

3 Of the 6,500 television channels available to EU and candidate countries in 2008, only 381 were terrestrial. Britons had access to most (883), followed by Germans (300). The Swedes, who had just two channels at the end of the 1980s, now had 136 (European Audiovisual Observatory, www.obs.coe.int).

4 The channels will be introduced in greater detail in the first chapter, and more will be said at the end of chapter 5 about the situating of 'traditional' television in the context of a changing media environment.

5 This is a stance shared by Silverstone (2007: 52, 80) and Hafez (2007: 10) among others.

Chapter 1 Introduction

1 Others, such as Heikkilä and Kunelius (2008), have explored the relationship between journalism and cosmopolitanism, but the concept is translated in their work into transnationalism at the EU level. What emerges from their analysis is an elite abstraction – a purely civic understanding – whereas the concern here is with cosmopolitanism that has a cultural as well as a political component and is interested not just in the EU but also in the world beyond it.

2 The term narrative can be so vague and encompassing that it is sometimes no use at all, according to some (Carlisle 1994: 1; see also Garme 2001: 27). One of the prime culprits here is Barthes ([1966] 1977: 79), who said, rather unhelpfully, that narrative was any form of communication: 'The narratives of the world are numberless. Narrative is first and foremost a prodigious variety of genres [. . .] narrative is international, transhistorical, transcultural: it is simply there, like life itself.' Not everyone bothers to define the term when they use it, which in narrative studies, as in all others, results in a good deal of confusion. But even those who do say what they have in mind do so in more or less concrete terms. Fredric Jameson, for example, takes narrative to be 'the central function or instance of the human mind' (cited in Carlisle 1994: 1), which is an intriguing thought, but hardly one that is of much assistance when trying to identify the occurrence of narratives in a given primary source material. On a similarly abstract level, Hayden White tells us that 'narrative is a metacode, a human universal on the basis of which transcultural messages about the nature of a shared reality can be transmitted' (White 1981: 1–2).

3 I am by no means alone in maintaining that television has a community-building function. Among those who argue along similar lines, or have written about news reporting in terms of storytelling, are Barkin (1984); Bell (1994); Bennett and Edelman (1985); Berger (1997); Bignell (1997); Birkvad (2000); Dahlgren (1995); Knight and Dean (1982); Kozloff (1992); Smith (1979); and Tuchman (1976).

Chapter 2 Reporting the World Back to Itself

1 Purely commercial channels, and US-based channels such as CNN, CNBC and Fox, were excluded from the study, as research on US

media has had a tendency to overshadow studies of news produced in European countries, and as an inquiry into cosmopolitanism made programmes with public service origins particularly interesting.

2 To the sample of nationally based broadcasters, one Spanish and one French channel are added in chapter 4. Spain is associated with the 'polarized pluralist' model, characterized by close ties between the media and the state and a weak public service tradition. According to Hallin and Mancini, France is a borderline case, usually placed in this model but with some features in common with the democratic corporatists: the importance of public service broadcasting is often emphasized, for example, but public funding has been relatively limited. The first French channel, TF1, was privatized in 1987 but as a member of the European Broadcasting Union is still considered a public broadcaster of sorts. Its 40 minute-long 8 p.m. broadcast, *Le journal de 20 heures*, is an institution in France and enjoys average ratings of 30 to 35 per cent. Spanish RTVE's *Telediario*, broadcasting 45 minutes of news daily at 9 p.m., is a long-running programme with 3 to 4 million viewers.

3 In the case of EuroNews, the rather problematic procedure was to place any news concerning an EU member state or the EU itself in this category.

Chapter 3 *The Woman with the Samsonite Suitcase*

1 Keynote speech by Nigel Chapman, director, BBC World Service, at the conference on 'International Broadcasting, Public Diplomacy and Cultural Exchange', School of Oriental and African Studies, London, 18 December 2007.

Chapter 4 *A Wave of Cosmopolitan Sentiment*

1 Kofi Annan on the BBC, 9 January 2005.

2 For technical reasons, one programme is missing from *Telediario* (Spanish), *Ten O'Clock News* (British) and EuroNews, and two from Deutsche Welle. All fifteen programmes in the sample period were analysed for all the other channels.

3 A large number of problems were coded for. In table 4.3, the results have been aggregated into problem categories. 'Human' problems

included dealing with dead and injured, controlling disease, identifying the dead, tracing missing persons, uncertainty over the fate of victims, dealing with traumatized survivors and getting people home. Among 'political' problems were failings of the government of the reporting country, failings of another government or authority and the lack of a warning system. 'Aid'-related problems took in getting aid through, destroyed infrastructure and logistical problems. 'Other' problems covered trafficking, theft, corruption and environmental problems.

4 The original coding resulted in a larger number of actor types, which were subsequently aggregated into the categories presented in table 4.4. The aggregate categories 'own country' and 'other country' include government, officials or other authorities. The category 'world community' covers references to the international community, the UN, the EU, 'the world', etc. The 'NGO' category includes aid agencies/workers, expert volunteers, psychologists, doctors and nurses. 'Ordinary people' means tourists, relatives, the man on the street and non-professional volunteers. Among the category 'other' are spiritual leaders, the business community, celebrities, royals – and elephants.

5 The 'own country' and afflicted country categories refer to the government, members of the government or other politicians, or the authorities, military or police in that country. The 'world community' category includes references to the international community, the UN, the EU, 'the world', etc. Here, 'NGOs' refers to organizations and aid agencies rather than people. The 'aid workers' category on the other hand refers to people rather than organizations and embraces professional volunteers, doctors, nurses, and so on. The 'ordinary people' category covers individuals from the countries hit by the tsunami and tourists, as well as individuals elsewhere in the world. The category entitled 'other' takes in businesses, spiritual leaders, celebrities, and so on.

6 BBC World, 1 January 2005.

Chapter 5 Old Wars in News Programmes

1 BBC, *10 O'Clock News*, 29 May 2004.
2 Ibid., 1 June 2004.
3 Ibid., 4 June 2004.
4 Mary Crofton, interviewed on SVT's *Rapport*, 6 June 2004.

5 Jean-Pierre Gueno, interviewed on BBC World News, 2 June 2004.
6 EuroNews, 18 May 2004.
7 Emmanuel Todd, interviewed on EuroNews, 1 June 2004.
8 French president Jacques Chirac on EuroNews, 6 June 2004.
9 EuroNews, 10 June 2004.

Chapter 6 Brushing away the Flies

1 The Sudan crisis, *Heute*, 31 May 2004.
2 Explaining what this involves is best done by responding to a narrative.
   Doing research is a matter of dialogue, both with the material being
   analysed and with other scholars (and, in this case, media consumers).
   For the dialogue to work, the analysis of the primary source material
   must be transparent: the researcher should take the reader by the hand,
   as it were, and lead him or her through the material that has been analysed in the way in which an experienced traveller might introduce a
   tourist to a city or landscape he or she has never visited before. While
   the experienced traveller (researcher) might have the advantage of
   knowing the place better than the tourist (reader), they should be able
   to have a dialogue between equals as to what to make of it. Perhaps
   the traveller, who has worshipped or attended concerts there dozens of
   times, asserts that the cathedral is a fine example of, say, Gothic architecture. The tourist, although looking at this particular building for
   the first time, could turn out to be an expert on cathedrals in another
   country, or on Gothic architecture in general, and is thus in a position to disagree with the traveller. Listening to the arguments of the
   tourist, the traveller realizes that she may have to reconsider the way
   she has been looking at the cathedral she thought she knew so well.
   The point of this story is that such a discussion cannot take place if the
   traveller/researcher does not take the tourist/reader to the place that
   is so familiar to her, and show it to him or her. Substituting the cathedral with 'primary sources' or 'text', this means that the dialogue on
   which good scholarship is based cannot take place unless the researcher
   shares those primary sources with the reader – puts all the cards on
   the table, as it were. When the primary source material is comprised
   of several hundred news broadcasts and more than 2,000 news items
   (and transcriptions of dozens of hours of interviews), in languages that
   may not always be accessible to the reader, the business of sharing – of

transparency in reporting results – is something of a challenge. As it has not been possible to find a publisher prepared to print a thousand-page book, and because of the unlikelihood of finding anyone prepared to read it, the material on which this book has been based has of necessity been presented in summary form – as a narrative of narratives.

3 Susan Stein, interviewed by Michael Buerk in the 1992 BBC documentary *Eye on the Storm*.

References and Bibliography

Abell, Peter (1987) *The Syntax of Social Life: The Theory and Method of Comparative Narrative*. Oxford: Oxford University Press.

Altheide, David L., and Robert P. Snow (1991) *Media Worlds in the Postjournalism Era*. New York: Aldine de Gruyter.

Andén-Papadopoulos, Kari (2008) 'The Abu Ghraib torture photographs: news frames, visual culture, and the power of images', *Journalism*, 9(1): 5–30.

Anderson, Benedict ([1983] 2006) *Imagined Communities*. London and New York: Verso.

Ang, Ien (1985) *Watching Dallas: Soap Opera and the Melodramatic Imagination*. London: Methuen.

Appadurai, Arjun (1996) *Modernity at Large: Cultural Dimensions of Globalization*. London: University of Minnesota Press.

Archetti, Cristina (2008) 'News coverage of 9/11 and the demise of the media flows, globalization and localization hypotheses', *International Communication Gazette*, 70: 463–85.

Archibugi, Daniele (ed.) (2003) *Debating Cosmopolitics*. London and New York: Verso.

Arendt, Hannah (1994) *Essays in Understanding, 1930–1954*, ed. Jerome Kohn. New York: Harcourt, Brace.

Ascherson, Neal (1988) *Games with Shadows*. London: Radius.

Ashuri, Tamar (2006) 'Television tension: national versus cosmopolitan memory in a co-produced television documentary', *Media, Culture & Society*, 29: 31–51.

Aumont, Jacques (1997) *The Image*. London: British Film Institute.

Baer, Alejandro (2001) 'Consuming history and memory through mass media products', *European Journal of Cultural Studies*, 4: 491–501.

Barker, Chris (1999) *Television, Globalization and Cultural Identities*. Buckingham: Open University Press.

Barkin, Steve M. (1984) 'The journalist as storyteller: an interdisciplinary perspective', *American Journalism* (winter): 27–33.

Barthes, Roland ([1966] 1977) 'Introduction to the structural analysis of narratives', in Roland Barthes, *Image–Music–Text*. London: Collins, pp. 79–124.

Barthes, Roland (1993) *Mythologies*. London: Vintage.

Beck, Ulrich (2006) *The Cosmopolitan Vision*. Cambridge: Polity.

Beck, Ulrich, and Natan Sznaider (2006) 'Unpacking cosmopolitanism for the social sciences: a research agenda', *British Journal of Sociology*, 57(1): 1–23.

Becker, Karin (1995) 'Media and the ritual process', *Media, Culture & Society*, 17: 629–46.

Bell, Allan (1994) 'Telling stories', in D. Graddol and O. Boyd-Barrett (eds), *Media Texts: Authors and Readers*. Clevedon: Multilingual Matters in association with the Open University, pp. 100–18.

Bell, Allan, and Peter Garrett (eds) (1998) *Approaches to Media Discourse*. Oxford: Blackwell.

Bell, Erin (2007) 'Televising history: the past(s) on the small screen', *European Journal of Cultural Studies*, 10: 5–12.

Bell, Erin, and Ann Gray (2007) 'History on television: charisma, narrative and knowledge', *European Journal of Cultural Studies* 10: 113–33.

Benhabib, Seyla (2004) *The Claims of Culture: Equality and Diversity in the Global Era*. Princeton, NJ: Princeton University Press.

Bennett, W. Lance, and Murray Edelman (1985) 'Toward a new political narrative', *Journal of Communication*, 35: 156–71.

Berger, Arthur Asa (1997) *Narratives in Popular Culture, Media and Everyday Life*. London: Sage.

Bhabha, Homi K. (ed.) (1990) *Nation and Narration*. London: Routledge.

Bignell, Jonathan (1997) *Media Semiotics: An Introduction*. Manchester: Manchester University Press.

Billig, Michael (1992) *Banal Nationalism*. London: Sage.

Bird, S. E. (1987) 'Media and folklore as intertextual communication processes: John F. Kennedy and the supermarket tabloids', in *Communication Yearbook* [New Brunswick, NJ], 10: 758–72.

Birkvad, Søren (2000) 'A battle for public mythology: history and genre in the portrait documentary', *Nordicom Review*, 21(2): 291–304.

Boltanski, Luc (1999) *Distant Suffering: Morality, Media and Politics*. Cambridge: Cambridge University Press.

Bondebjerg, Ib (1992) 'Intertextuality and metafiction: genre and narration in the television fiction of Dennis Potter', in Michael Skovmand and Kim Christian Schrøder (eds), *Media Cultures: Reappraising Transnational Media*. London: Routledge, pp. 161–80.

Boulding, Kenneth (1959) 'National images and international systems', *Conflict Resolution*, 3(2): 120–31.

Boyd-Barrett, Oliver (1994) 'Language and media: a question of convergence', in David Graddol and Oliver Boyd-Barrett (eds), *Media Texts: Authors and Readers*. Clevedon: Multilingual Matters in association with the Open University, pp. 22–39.

Bremond, Claude ([1966] 1980) 'The logic of narrative possibilities', *New Literary History*, 11: 387–411.

Brennan, Timothy (2002) 'Cosmo-theory', *South Atlantic Quarterly*, 100: 659–91.

Brennan, Timothy (2003) 'Cosmopolitanism and internationalism', in Daniele Archibugi (ed.), *Debating Cosmopolitics*. London: Verso, pp. 40–50.

Brewer, Paul R. (2006) 'National interest frames and public opinion about world affairs', *Press/Politics*, 11(4): 89–102.

Brinker, Menachem (1983) 'Verisimilitude, conventions and beliefs', *New Literary History*, 14: 253–67.

Brundson, Charlotte, and David Morley (1978) *Everyday Television: Nationwide*. London: British Film Institute.

Brune, Ylva (2004) *Nyheter från Gränsen: tre studier i journalistik om 'invandrare', flytkningar och rasistiskt våld*. Gothenburg: JMG.

Bruner, Jerome (1991) 'The narrative construction of reality', *Critical Inquiry*, 18: 1–21.

Calabrese, Andrew (2007) 'Historical memory, media studies and journalism ethics', *Global Media and Communication*, 3: 363–70.

Calhoun, Craig (2002) 'The class consciousness of frequent travelers: toward a critique of actually existing cosmopolitanism', *South Atlantic Quarterly*, 101: 869–97.

Calhoun, Craig (2004) 'A world of emergencies: fear, intervention, and the limits of cosmopolitan order', *Canadian Review of Sociology and Anthropology*, 41: 373–95.

Carey, James W. (1989) *Communication as Culture: Essays on Media and Society*. London: Routledge.

Carlisle, Janice (1994) 'Introduction', in Janice Carlisle and Daniel R. Schwarz (eds), *Narrative and Culture*. London: University of Georgia Press, pp. 1–12.

Castells, Manuel (1996) *The Information Age: Economy, Society and Culture*, Vol. 1: *The Rise of the Network Society*. Oxford: Blackwell.

Castells, Manuel (1997) *The Information Age: Economy, Society and Culture*, Vol. 2: *The Power of Identity*. Oxford: Blackwell.

Chalaby, Jean K. (ed.) (2005) *Transnational Television Worldwide: Towards a New Media Order*. London: I. B. Tauris.

Chalaby, Jean K. (2007) 'Beyond nation-centrism: thinking international communication from a cosmopolitan perspective', *Studies in Communication Sciences*, 7(1): 61–83.

Chaney, David (1986) 'A symbolic mirror of ourselves: civic ritual in mass society', in Richard Collins et al. (eds), *Media, Culture and Society: A Critical Reader*. London: Sage.

Chapman, James (2007) 'Re-presenting war: British television drama-documentary and the Second World War', *European Journal of Cultural Studies*, 10: 13–33.

Chatman, Seymour (1978) *Story and Discourse: Narrative Structure in Fiction and Film*. Ithaca, NY, and London: Cornell University Press.

Chatman, Seymour (1990) *Coming to Terms: The Rhetoric of Narrative in Fiction and Film*. Ithaca, NY: Cornell University Press.

Cheah, Pheng, and Bruce Robbins (eds) (1998) *Cosmopolitics: Thinking and Feeling beyond the Nation*. Minneapolis and London: University of Minnesota Press.

Chouliaraki, Lilie (2006) *The Spectatorship of Suffering*. London: Sage.

Chouliaraki, Lilie (2008) 'The symbolic power of transnational media', *Global Media and Communication*, 4: 329–51.

Clausen, Lisbeth (2004) 'Localizing the global: "domestication" processes in international news production', *Media, Culture & Society*, 26: 25–44.

Clayton, Jay (1994) 'The narrative turn in minority fiction', in Janice Carlisle and Daniel R. Schwarz (eds), *Narrative and Culture*. London: University of Georgia Press, pp. 58–76.

Cohen, Akiba A., Mark R. Levy, Itzhak Roeh and Michael Gurevitch (1996) *Global Newsrooms, Local Audiences: A Study of the Eurovision News Exchange*. London: John Libbey.

Cohen, Bernard (1963) *The Press and Foreign Policy*. Princeton, NJ: Princeton University Press.

Coole, Diana (1999) 'Narrative, maps and the theatre of politics', paper presented at the ECPR Joint Sessions of Workshops, Mannheim.

Corner, John, and Kay Richardson (2008) 'Political culture and television fiction: the Amazing Mrs Pritchard', *European Journal of Cultural Studies*, 11: 387–403.

Cottle, Simon (2006) *Mediatized Conflict*. Maidenhead: Open University Press.

Cottle, Simon (2009) *Global Crisis Reporting: Journalism in the Global Age*. Maidenhead: Open University Press.

Cottle, Simon, and Mugdha Rai (2008) 'Global 24/7 news providers: emissaries of global dominance or global public service?', *Global Media and Communication*, 4: 157–81.

Couldry, Nick (2007) 'Researching media internationalization: comparative media research as if we really meant it', *Global Media and Communication*, 3: 247–71.

Czarniawska, Barbara (1999) *Interviews, Narratives and Organizations*. Gothenburg: GRI.

Czarniawska, Barbara (2000) *The Use of Narrative in Organization Research*, Report 2000/5. Gothenburg: GRI.

Czarniawska, Barbara (2004) *Narratives in Social Science Research*. London: Sage.

Dahlgren, Peter (1988) 'What's the meaning of this? Viewers' plural sense-making of TV news', *Media, Culture & Society*, 10: 285–301.

Dahlgren, Peter (1995) *Television and the Public Sphere: Citizenship, Democracy and the Media*. London: Sage.

Dayan, Daniel, and Elihu Katz (1992) *Media Events: The Live Broadcasting of History*. Cambridge, MA, and London: Harvard University Press.

De Leeuw, Sonja (2007) 'Dutch documentary film as a site of memory: changing perspectives in the 1990s', *European Journal of Cultural Studies*, 10: 75–87.

Delanty, Gerhard (2003) *Community*. London: Routledge.

Delanty, Gerhard (2006) 'The cosmopolitan imagination: critical cosmopolitanism and social theory', *British Journal of Sociology*, 57(1): 25–47.

Delgado, Fernando (2003) 'The fusing of sport and politics: media constructions of US versus Iran at France '98', *Journal of Sport and Social Issues*, 27: 293–307.

Devereux, Eoin (2003) *Understanding the Media*. London: Sage.

Dhoest, Alexander (2007) 'Identifying with the nation: viewer memories of Flemish TV fiction', *European Journal of Cultural Studies*, 10: 55–73.

Dine, Philip (1994) *Images of the Algerian War: French Fiction and Film, 1954–1992*. Oxford: Oxford University Press.

Dryzek, John (2000) *Deliberative Democracy and Beyond*. Oxford: Oxford University Press.

Durham, Frank (2008) 'Media ritual in catastrophic time: the populist turn in television coverage of Hurricane Katrina', *Journalism*, 9: 95–116.

Ebbrecht, Tobias (2007) 'Docudramatizing history on TV: German and British docudrama and historical event evaluation in the memorial year 2005', *European Journal of Cultural Studies*, 10: 35–53.

Ekdal, Niklas (2004) 'De onda, de goda och de fula', *Dagens Nyheter*, 11 January, p. A02.

Elliot, Deni (1989) 'Tales from the darkside: ethical implications of disaster coverage', in L. M. Walters, L. Wilkins and T. Walters (eds), *Bad Tidings: Communication and Catastrophe*. Hillsdale, NJ: Lawrence Erlbaum Associates, pp. 161–70.

Elliot, Philip (1982) 'Press performance as political ritual', in D. C. Whitney, E. Wartella and S. Windahl (eds), *Mass Communication Yearbook 3*, pp. 583–619.

Elliot, Philip, Graham Murdock and Philip Schlesinger (1986) '"Terrorism" and the state: a case study of the discourses of television', in Richard Collins et al. (eds), *Media, Culture and Society: A Critical Reader*. London: Sage.

Ettema, James S. (2005) 'Crafting cultural resonance: imaginative power in everyday journalism', *Journalism*, 6: 131–52.

Fahmy, Shahira, and Daekyung Kim (2008) 'Picturing the Iraq War: constructing the image of war in the British and US Press', *International Communication Gazette*, 70: 443–62.

Fairclough, Norman (1995) *Media Discourse*. London: Edward Arnold.

Featherstone, Mike (1995) *Undoing Culture: Globalization, Postmodernism and Identity*. London: Sage.

Fisher, Walter (1984) 'Narrative as a human communication paradigm: the case of public moral argument', *Communication Monographs* 52: 347–67.

Fishman, Ethan (1989) *Likely Stories: Essays on Political Philosophy and Contemporary American Literature*. Gainsville: University of Florida Press.

Fiske, John ([1987] 1995) *Television Culture*. London: Routledge.

Fiske, John, and John Hartley (1978) *Reading Television*. London: Methuen.

Fowler, Roger (1991) *Language in the News: Discourse and Ideology in the Press*. London: Routledge.

Frosch, Paul, and Wolfsfeld, G. (2006) 'ImagiNation: news discourse, nationhood and civil society', *Media, Culture & Society*, 29: 105–29.

Galloway, Steven (2008) *The Cellist of Sarajevo*. London: Atlantic Books.

Galtung, Johan, and Mari Ruge (1965) 'The structure of foreign news: the presentation of the Congo, Cuba and Cyprus crises in four newspapers', *Journal of International Peace Research* 1: 64–90.

Garme, Cecilia (2001) *Newcomers to Power: How to Sit on Someone Else's Throne: Socialists Conquer France in 1981, Non-Socialists Conquer Sweden in 1976*. Acta Universitatis Uppsaliensis, Skrifter utgivna av Statsvetenskapliga föreningen i Uppsala, 148.

Giddens, Anthony (1991) *Modernity and Self-Identity: Self and Society in the Late Modern Age*. Cambridge: Polity.

Gitlin, Todd (1980) *The Whole World is Watching*. Berkeley: University of California Press.

Gjedde, Lisa (2000) 'Narrative, genre and context in popular science', *Nordicom Review*, 21(1): 51–7.

Graddol, David (1994) 'The visual accomplishment of factuality', in D. Graddol and O. Boyd-Barrett (eds), *Media Texts: Authors and Readers*. Clevedon: Multilingual Matters in association with the Open University, pp. 136–57.

Gray, Martin (1992) *A Dictionary of Literary Terms*. Harlow: Longman.

Gurevitch, Michael (1996) 'The globalization of electronic journalism', in James Curran and Michael Gurevitch (eds), *Mass Media and Society*. London: Arnold, pp. 204–33.

Habermas, Jürgen (2001) *The Postnational Constellation: Political Essays*. Cambridge: Polity.

Hafez, Kai (2007) *The Myth of Media Globalization*. Cambridge: Polity.

Hall, Stuart (1992) 'The West and the rest: discourse and power', in Stuart Hall and Bram Gieben (eds), *Formations of Modernity*. Cambridge: Polity in association with the Open University, pp. 275–331.

Hall, Stuart (1994) 'Encoding/decoding', in D. Graddol and O. Boyd-Barrett (eds), *Media Texts: Authors and Readers*. Clevedon: Multilingual Matters in association with the Open University, pp. 200–11.

Hall, Stuart (1997) 'The work of representation', in Stuart Hall (ed.), *Representation: Cultural Representations and Signifying Practices*. London: Sage and Open University Press, pp. 13–64.

Hallin, Daniel C., and Paolo Mancini (2004) *Comparing Media Systems: Three Models of Media and Politics*. Cambridge: Cambridge University Press.

Hannerz, Ulf (1990) 'Cosmopolitans and locals in world culture', *Theory, Culture and Society*, 7: 237–51.

Hannerz, Ulf (1996) *Transnational Connections*. London: Routledge.

Hannerz, Ulf (2004a) 'Cosmopolitanism', in David Nugent and Joan Vincent (eds), *A Companion to the Anthropology of Politics*. Oxford: Blackwell, pp. 69–85.

Hannerz, Ulf (2004b) *Foreign News: Exploring the World of Foreign Correspondents*. Chicago: University of Chicago Press.

Hannerz, Ulf (2005) 'Two faces of cosmopolitanism: culture and politics', *Statsvetenskaplig tidskrift*, 107(3): 199–213.

Hartley, John ([1982] 1995) *Understanding the News*. London: Routledge.

Harvey, D. (1990) *The Condition of Postmodernity*. Oxford: Blackwell.

Heer, Hannes, Walter Manoschek, Alexander Pollack and Ruth Wodak (eds) (2008) *The Discursive Construction of History: Remembering the Wehrmacht's War of Annihilation*. Basingstoke: Palgrave Macmillan.

Heikkilä, Heikki, and Risto Kunelius (2008) 'Ambivalent ambassadors and realistic reporters', *Journalism*, 9: 377–97.

Held, David (2002) 'Cosmopolitanism: ideas, realities and deficits', in David Held and Anthony McGrew (eds), *Governing Globalization: Power, Authority and Global Governance*. Cambridge: Polity, pp. 305–23.

Herzog, Annabel (1999) 'The poetic nature of political disclosure: Hannah Arendt's storytelling', paper presented at the ECPR Joint Sessions of Workshops, Mannheim.

Höijer, B. (2004) 'The discourse of global compassion: the audience and media reporting of human suffering', *Media, Culture & Society*, 26: 513–31.

Holton, Robert J. (2009) *Cosmopolitanisms: New Thinking and New Directions*. Basingstoke and New York: Palgrave Macmillan.

Huxford, John (2007) 'The proximity paradox: live reporting, virtual proximity and the concept of place in the news', *Journalism*, 8: 657–74.

Hyvärinen, Matti (1999) 'Narrating the nation: *Seven Brothers* envision Finland', paper presented at the ECPR Joint Sessions of Workshops, Mannheim.

Hyvärinen, Matti (2000) 'Epistemological, ontological and constructive perspectives on political narrativity', paper presented at the IPSA World Congress, Québec City.

Jameson, Fredric (1981) *The Political Unconscious: Narrative as a Social Symbolic Act*. Ithaca, NY: Cornell University Press.

Jensen, Klaus Bruhn (1995) *The Social Semiotics of Mass Communication*. London: Sage.

Jensen, Klaus Bruhn (ed.) (2002) *A Handbook of Media and Communication Research*. London: Routledge.

Kiser, Edgar (1996) 'The revival of narrative in historical sociology: what rational choice theory can contribute', *Politics & Society*, 24: 249–71.

Kitzinger, Jenny (2000) 'Media templates: patterns of association and the (re)construction of meaning over time', *Media, Culture & Society*, 22: 61–84.

Knight, Graham, and Dean, Tony (1982) 'Myth and the structure of news', *Journal of Communication*, 32: 144–61.

Kozloff, Sara (1992) 'Narrative theory and television', in Robert C. Allen (ed.), *Channels of Discourse, Reassembled: Television and Contemporary Criticism*. London: Routledge, pp. 67–100.

Labov, William, and Waletzky, Joshua (1967) 'Narrative analysis: oral versions of personal experience', in June Helm (ed.), *Essays on Verbal and Visual Arts*. Seattle: University of Washington Press.

Lagerkvist, Amanda (2004) '"We see America": mediatized and mobile gazes in Swedish post-war travelogues', *International Journal of Cultural Studies*, 7: 321–42.

Lancaster, Thomas D. (1999) 'The narration of politics: literary illumination of collective action problems', paper presented at the ECPR Joint Sessions of Workshops, Mannheim.

Larsen, Peter (2002) 'Mediated fiction', in Klaus Bruhn Jensen (ed.), *A Handbook of Media and Communications Research*. London: Routledge, pp. 117–37.

Lazarsfeld, Paul (1941) 'Remarks on communication research', *Studies in Philosophy and Social Science*, 9(1): 2–16.

Lévi-Strauss, Claude (1963) 'The structural study of myth', in *Structural Anthropology*. Harmondsworth: Penguin, pp. 206–31.

Levy, D., and N. Sznaider (2002) 'Memory unbound: the Holocaust and the formation of cosmopolitan memory', *European Journal of Social Theory*, 5(1): 87–106.

Lewis, Justin, Sanna Inthorn and Karin Wahl-Jorgensen (2005) *Citizens or Consumers? What the Media Tell Us about Political Participation*. Maidenhead: Open University Press.

Liebes, Tamar (1994) 'Narrativization of the news', *Journal of Narrative and Life History*, 4(1&2): 1–8.

Liebes, Tamar, and Elihu Katz (1991) *The Export of Meaning*. Oxford: Oxford University Press.

Lieblich, Amia, Rivka Tuval-Mashiach and Tamar Zilber (1998) *Narrative Research: Reading, Analysis and Interpretation*. Thousand Oaks, CA, and London: Sage.

Loshitzky, Yosefa (1996) 'Travelling culture/travelling television', *Screen*, 37: 323–35.

Lull, James (2007) *Culture-on-Demand: Communication in a Crisis World*. Oxford: Blackwell.

Lyotard, Jean-François (1984) *The Postmodern Condition: A Report on Knowledge*. Minneapolis: University of Minnesota Press.

McAdams, Dan P. (1993) *The Stories We Live By: Personal Myths and the Making of the Self*. New York: Guilford Press.

MacBride, Seán (1980) *Many Voices, One World*. Paris: Unesco.

Machill, Marcel (1998) 'EuroNews: the first European news channel as a case study for media industry development in Europe and for spectra of transnational journalism research', *Media, Culture & Society*, 20: 427–50.

Machill, Marcel, Sebastian Köhler and Markus Waldhauser (2007) 'The use of narrative structures in television news: an experiment in innovative forms of journalistic presentation', *European Journal of Communication*, 22: 185–205.

Mackay, Hugh, and Tim O'Sullivan (eds) (1999) *The Media Reader: Continuity and Transformation*. London: Sage.

McMillan, Divya C. (2007) *International Media Studies*. Oxford: Blackwell.

Mandelbaum, Maurice (1967) 'A note on history as narrative', *History and Theory*, 6: 413–19.

Manning, Peter K., and Betsy Cullum-Swan (1994) 'Narrative, content, and semiotic analysis', in N. K. Denzin and Y. S. Lincoln (eds), *Handbook of Qualitative Research*. London: Sage, pp. 463–77.

Martin, Vivian B. (2008) 'Attending the news: a grounded theory about a daily regimen', *Journalism*, 9: 76–94.

Martin, Wallace (1986) *Recent Theories of Narrative*. Ithaca, NY, and London: Cornell University Press.

Meyrowitz, Joshua (1999) 'No sense of place: the impact of electronic media on social behavior', in Hugh Mackay and Tim O'Sullivan (eds), *The Media Reader: Continuity and Transformation*. London: Sage and Open University Press, pp. 99–120.

Mihelj, Sabina (2008) 'National media events: from displays of unity to enactments of division', *European Journal of Cultural Studies*, 11: 471–88.

Miller, J. Hillis (1974) 'Narrative and history', *Journal of English Literary History*, 41: 455–73.

Mink, Louise (1978) 'Narrative form as a cognitive instrument', in Robert Canary and Henry Kozicki (eds), *The Writing of History: Literary Form and Historical Understanding*. Madison: University of Wisconsin Press, pp. 129–49.

Moeller, Susan D. (1999) *Compassion Fatigue: How the Media Sell Disease, Famine, War and Death*. London: Routledge.

Moon, Claire (1999) 'True fictions: truth, reconciliation, and the narrativisation of identity', paper presented at the ECPR Joint Sessions of Workshops, Mannheim.

Morley, David (1980) *The Nationwide Audience*. London: British Film Institute.

Morley, David (1992) 'Electronic communities and domestic rituals: cultural consumption and the production of European cultural identities', in Michael Skovmand and Kim Christian Schrøder (eds), *Media Cultures: Reappraising Transnational Media*. London: Routledge, pp. 65–83.

Morley, David, and Kevin Robins (1995) *Spaces of Identity: Global Media, Electronic Landscapes and Cultural Boundaries*. London: Routledge.

Mottier, Véronique (1999) 'Narratives of national identity: sexuality, race, and the Swiss "dream of order"', paper presented at the ECPR Joint Sessions of Workshops, Mannheim.

Mumby, Dennis K. (1993) *Narrative and Social Control: Critical Perspectives*. London: Sage.

Murray, Craig, Katy Parry, Piers Robinson and Peter Goddard (2008) 'Reporting dissent in wartime: British press, the anti-war movement and the 2003 Iraq War', *European Journal of Communication*, 23(1): 7–27.

Nash, Christopher (ed.) (1994) *Narrative in Culture: The Uses of Storytelling in the Sciences, Philosophy and Literature*. London: Routledge.

Nava, Mica (2007) *Visceral Cosmopolitanism: Gender, Culture and the Normalisation of Difference*. Oxford and New York: Berg.

Nederveen Pieterse, Jan (1995) 'Globalisation as hybridisation', in M. Featherstone, S. Lash and R. Robertson (eds), *Global Modernities*. London: Sage, pp. 45–68.

Nederveen Pieterse, Jan (2004) *Globalization and Culture: Global Mélange*. Oxford: Rowman & Littlefield.

Negrine, Ralph (1996) *The Communication of Politics*. London: Sage.

Neveu, Eric, and Franca Roncarolo (1999) 'The political uses of politicians' (auto)biographies: a comparative study: France and Italy', paper presented at the ECPR Joint Sessions of Workshops, Mannheim.

Novais, Rui Alexandre (2007) 'National influences in foreign news: British and Portuguese press coverage of the Dili massacre in East Timor', *International Communication Gazette*, 69: 553–73.

Nussbaum, Martha C. (1996) *For Love of Country: Debating the Limits of Patriotism*, ed. Joshua Cohen. Boston: Beacon Press.

O'Sullivan, Tim, Brian Dutton and Philip Rayner (1994) *Studying the Media*. London: Edward Arnold.

Owen, Susan (1993) 'Oppositional voices in *China Beach*: narrative configurations of gender and war', in D. K. Mumby (ed.), *Narrative and Social Control: Critical Perspectives*. London: Sage, pp. 207–31.

Pantti, Mervi (2005) 'Masculine tears, feminine tears – and crocodile tears: mourning Olof Palme and Anna Lindh in Finnish newspapers', *Journalism*, 6: 357–77.

Papacharissi, Zizi, and Maria de Fatima Oliveira (2008) 'News frames terrorism: a comparative analysis of frames employed in terrorism coverage in US and UK newspapers', *Press/Politics*, 13(1): 52–74.

Peffley, Mark, and Jon Hurwitz (1992) 'International events and foreign policy beliefs: public response to changing Soviet–US relations', *American Journal of Political Science*, 36: 431–61.

Polkinghorne, Donald E. (1987) *Narrative Knowing and the Human Sciences.* Albany: State University of New York Press.

Preston, Peter (1997) *Political/Cultural Identity: Citizens and Nations in a Global Era.* London: Sage.

Price, Monroe (1995) *Television, the Public Sphere and National Identity.* Oxford: Clarendon Press.

Propp, Vladimir ([1928] 1968) *Morphology of the Folktale.* Austin: University of Texas Press.

Quarantelli, Enrico L. (1989) 'The social science study of disasters and mass communication', in L. M. Walters, L. Wilkins and T. Walers (eds), *Bad Tidings: Communication and Catastrophe.* Hillsdale, NJ: Lawrence Erlbaum Associates, pp. 1–20.

Rantanen, Terhi (2005) *The Media and Globalization.* London: Sage.

Richardson, Kay, and Ulrike H. Meinhof (1999) *Worlds in Common? Television Discourse in a Changing Europe.* London: Routledge.

Riessman, Catherine Kohler (1993) *Narrative Analysis.* Newbury Park, CA, and London: Sage.

Robertson, Alexa (1999) 'Kommunikation i den globala byn: mass-medierna och internationalisering', in K. Goldmann, J. Hallenberg, B. Jacobsson, Mörth and A. Robertson, *Politikens internationalisering.* Lund: Studentlitteratur.

Robertson, Alexa (2000) 'Europa erzählt: Erzählanalyse und Fernsehnachrichten über Europa', in J. W. Deth and T. König (eds), *Europäische Politikwissenschaft: Ein Blick in die Werkstatt.* Frankfurt: Campus.

Robertson, Alexa (2002) 'Narrativanalys och identitetsforskning', in Bo Petersson and Alexa Robertson (eds), *Identitetsforskning i praktiken.* Stockholm: Liber.

Robertson, Alexa (2005) 'Narrativanalys', in Göran Bergström and Kristina Boréus (eds), *Textens mening och makt.* 2nd edn, Lund: Studentlitteratur, pp. 219–62.

Robertson, Alexa (2008) 'Cosmopolitanization and real time tragedy: television news coverage of the Asian tsunami', *New Global Studies*, 2(2): article 3; available at www.bepress.com/ngs/vol2/iss2/art3.

Robertson, Alexa (2010) 'Euromedia: integration and cultural diversity in a changing media landscape', in Thomas McPhail (ed.), *Global Communication.* 3rd edn, Oxford: Wiley-Blackwell.

Roudometof, Victor (2005) 'Transnationalism, cosmopolitanism and glocalization', *Current Sociology*, 53(1): 113–35.

Rowe, John Carlos (1994) 'Spin-off: the rhetoric of television and post-modern memory', in Janice Carlisle and Daniel R. Schwarz (eds), *Narrative and Culture*. London: University of Georgia Press.

Ruddock, Andy (2001) *Understanding Audiences: Theory and Method*. London: Sage.

Sanders, Karen (2003) *Ethics and Journalism*. London: Sage.

Schirato, Tony, and Jen Webb (2003) *Understanding Globalization*. London: Sage.

Schirmer, Dietmar (1993) 'The site of the "common European house": how a symbol structures political discourse', in Marc Abélès and Werner Rossade (eds), *Politique symbolique en Europe/Symbolische Politik in Europa*. Berlin: Duncker & Humbolt.

Schlesinger, Philip (1997) 'From cultural defence to political culture: media, politics and collective identity in the European Union', *Media, Culture & Society*, 19: 369–91.

Schudson, M. (1994) 'Culture and the integration of national societies', in D. Crane (ed.), *The Sociology of Culture: Emerging Theoretical Perspectives*. Oxford: Blackwell, pp. 21–4.

Seaton, Jean (2003) 'Understanding not empathy', in Dayan K. Thussu and Des Freedman (eds), *War and the Media*. London: Sage, pp. 45–54.

Shapiro, Michael J. (1988) *The Politics of Representation: Writing Practices in Biography, Photography and Policy Analysis*. Madison and London: University of Wisconsin Press.

Shell, Marc (1993) *Children of the Earth: Literature, Politics and Nationhood*. Oxford: Oxford University Press.

Silverstone, Roger (1984) 'Narrative strategies in television science: a case study', *Media, Culture & Society*, 6: 377–410.

Silverstone, Roger (2007) *Media and Morality: On the Rise of the Mediapolis*. Cambridge: Polity.

Smith, Anthony (1990) 'Towards a global culture?', *Theory, Culture & Society*, 7: 171–91.

Smith, Robert Rutherford (1979) 'Mythic elements in television news', *Journal of Communication* (winter): 75–82.

Somers, Margaret R. (1994) 'The narrative constitution of identity: a relational and network approach', *Theory and Society*, 23: 605–49.

Sommer, Doris (1991) *Foundational Fictions: The National Romances of Latin America*. Berkeley: University of California Press.

Stephenson, Susan (1999) 'Narrative, identity and modernity', paper presented at the ECPR Joint Sessions of Workshops, Mannheim.

Stevenson, Nick (1995) *Understanding Media Cultures*. London: Sage.

Stevenson, Nick (1999) *The Transformation of the Media: Globalization, Morality and Ethics*. London: Longman.

Stevenson, Nick (2003) *Cultural Citizenship: Cosmopolitan Questions*. Maidenhead: Open University Press.

Stokes, Jane (2003) *How to Do Media and Cultural Studies*. London: Sage.

Street, John (2001) *Mass Media, Politics and Democracy*. Basingstoke: Palgrave.

Sturken, M. (1997) *Tangled Memories: The Vietnam War, the AIDS Epidemic, and the Politics of Remembering*. Berkeley: University of California Press.

SVT (Sveriges Television) (2006) *Policy for Ethnic and Cultural Diversity within SVT 2006*, http://svt.se/content/l/c6/32/42/79/policy2006.pdf.

Szerszynski, Bronislaw, and John Urry (2002) 'Cultures of cosmopolitanism', *Sociological Review*, 50: 461–81.

Szerszynski, Bronislaw, and John Urry (2006) 'Visuality, mobility and the cosmopolitan: inhabiting the world from afar', *British Journal of Sociology*, 57(1): 113–31.

Tambling, Jeremy (1991) *Narrative and Ideology*. Milton Keynes: Open University Press.

Thompson, John (1995) *The Media and Modernity*. Cambridge: Polity.

Thompson, Kenneth (1997) *Media and Cultural Regulation*. London: Sage and Open University Press.

Thussu, Daya Kishan, and Des Freedman (eds) (2003) *War and the Media: Reporting Conflict 24/7*. London: Sage.

Tomlinson, John (1999) *Globalization and Culture*. Cambridge: Polity.

Tuchman, Gaye (1976) 'Telling stories', *Journal of Communication*, 26(4): 93–7.

Turner, Graeme (1994) 'Film languages', in David Graddol and Oliver Boyd-Barrett (eds), *Media Texts: Authors and Readers*. Clevedon: Multilingual Matters in association with the Open University, pp. 119–35.

Van Dijk, Teun (1988) *News Analysis: Case Studies of International and National News in the Press*. Hillsdale, NJ: Lawrence Erlbaum.

Van Dijk, Teun (1993) 'Stories and racism', in D. K. Mumby (ed.), *Narrative and Social Control: Critical Perspectives*. London: Sage, pp. 121–42.

Van Ginneken, Jaap (1998) *Understanding Global News*. London: Sage.

Vertovic, Steven, and Robin Cohen (eds) (2002) *Conceiving Cosmopolitanism: Theory, Context and Practice*. Oxford: Oxford University Press.

Volkmer, Ingrid (2005) 'News in the global public space', in Stuart Allan (ed.), *Journalism: Critical Issues*. Maidenhead: Open University Press, pp. 357–68.

Waisbord, Silvio (2008) 'News coverage of the Darfur conflict: a conversation with Jan Eliasson, United Nations special envoy to Dafur', *Press/Politics*, 13(1): 75–80.

Walzer, Michael (1994) *Thick and Thin: Moral Argument at Home and Abroad*. Notre Dame, IN, and London: University of Notre Dame Press.

Weinblatt, Karen Tenenboim (2008) 'Fighting for the story's life: nonclosure in journalistic narrative', *Journalism*, 9: 31–51.

Wells, Karen (2007) 'Narratives of liberation and narratives of innocent suffering: the rhetorical uses of images of Iraqi children in the British press', *Visual Communication*, 6(1): 55–71.

White, Hayden (1981) 'The value of narrativity in the representation of reality', in W. J. T. Mitchell (ed.), *On Narrative*. Chicago: University of Chicago Press, pp. 1–25.

White, Hayden (1984) 'The question of narrative in contemporary historical theory', *History and Theory*, 23: 1–33.

White, Hayden (1987) *The Content of the Form: Narrative Discourse and Historical Representation*. Baltimore: Johns Hopkins University Press.

Whitebrook, Maureen (1995) *Real Toads in Imaginary Gardens: Narrative Accounts of Liberalism*. Lanham, MD, and London: Rowman & Littlefield.

Whitebrook, Maureen (2001) *Identity, Narrative and Politics*. London: Routledge.

Wieten, Jan, Graham Murdock and Peter Dahlgren (eds) (2000) *Television across Europe*. London: Sage.

Wilkins, Lee (1985) 'Television and newspaper coverage of a blizzard: is the message helplessness?', *Newspaper Research Journal*, 6(4): 50–65.

Wilkins, Lee (1989) 'Bhopal: the politics of mediated risk', in L. M. Walters, L. Wilkins and T. Walters (eds), *Bad Tidings: Communication and Catastrophe*. Hillsdale, NJ: Lawrence Erlbaum Associates, pp. 21–34.

Winslade, John, Gerald Monk and Alison Cotte (1998) 'A narrative approach to the practice of mediation', *Negotiation Journal*, 14(1): 21–41.

Wood, Nancy (1991) 'The Holocaust: historical memories and contemporary identities', *Media, Culture & Society*, 13: 357–79.

Zelizer, Barbie (1993) 'American journalists and the death of Lee Harvey Oswald: narratives of self-legitimation', in D. K. Mumby (ed.), *Narrative and Social Control: Critical Perspectives*. London: Sage, pp. 189–20.

Index